✓

choices

for the high school graduate

Third Edition

A Survival Guide
for the Information Age

Bryna J. Fireside

Ferguson Publishing Company
Chicago, Illinois

Editor: Andrew Morkes
Proofreader: Bonnie Needham
Indexer: Sandi Schroeder
Interior Design: Joe Grossmann, Grossmann Consulting & Design

Library of Congress Cataloging-in-Publication Data
Fireside, Bryna J.
    Choices for the high school graduate: a survival guide for the
    information age/by Bryna Fireside. -- 3rd ed.
        p.   cm.
    Includes bibliographical references (p.   ) and index.
    ISBN 0-89434-277-0
    1. Student aspirations--Handbooks, manuals, etc. 2. Student
    aspirations--United States--Handbooks, manuals, etc.
    3. Vocational guidance--United States--Handbooks, manuals,
    etc. 4. College student orientation--United States--
    Handbooks, manuals, etc. 5. Career development--United
    States--Handbooks, manuals, etc.
    I. Title
    LB1027.8.F58   1999
    373.18'0973--dc21
                                                    99-14052
                                                        CIP

Published and distributed by
Ferguson Publishing Company
312/580-5480
Web site: http://www.fergpubco.com

Printed in the United States of America
W-3

DEDICATION

For Harvey Fireside, with whom I
continue to share so many great adventures.

ABOUT THE AUTHOR

Bryna J. Fireside has been an educator and social activist for most of her life. Trained as a teacher, she earned a BA in English from Rutgers University and an MA in Education from Cornell University. She has taught public school in Chicago, Baltimore, and New York City. She also taught part-time in the Interdisciplinary Studies Department at Ithaca College, and supervised student teachers at SUNY Cortland.

In addition to teaching, she has published over 250 articles and book reviews in various national magazines and newspapers, including *Seventeen, The New York Times Metro* section, *The New York Times Book Review,* and *Education Life.*

She is the author of several books for young readers, including *Young People From Bosnia Talk About War* (Enslow), *Is There a Woman in the House . . . or Senate?* (Albert Whitman), and *Special Parents, Special Children* (Albert Whitman).

ACKNOWLEDGMENTS

It was my good fortune to interview dozens of young people for this book. Thank you one and all for taking the time to share your experiences with me. I only wish that I could have used all the stories I collected, but alas! that just wasn't possible. I deeply appreciate the time given me by college administrators and by the people who direct many of the organizations mentioned in this book. A special thanks to Peter Francese, president of *American Demographics Magazine* for his concise and insightful comments on what kinds of careers are going to be in demand for you who are soon to graduate high school and are considering your options. Thanks, too, to Dr. Carl Haynes, president of Tompkins-Cortland Community College for sharing some of the exciting new developments as community colleges retool for the Information Age.

And finally, I thank my own three children who managed to give me numerous heart-stopping moments as they tore through their "terrible teens." They each made their way into adulthood with a surprising amount of smarts, good sense, and social conscience. Were it not for their daring to break the rules of traditional lock-step education, I would not have dared to write this book.

TABLE OF CONTENTS

"In This Rapidly Changing Environment If You're Not Confused, You're Not Thinking Clearly"—Burt Nanus, author of The Leader's Edge : The Seven Keys to Leadership in a Turbulent World

SEVERAL YEARS AGO I INTERVIEWED DOZENS OF YOUNG PEOPLE, college administrators, parents, and teachers for a book I called *Choices: A Student Survival Guide for the 1990s.* I hoped that by letting young adults talk about their quest they would help others see that it isn't always necessary or right to accept someone else's notion of how to grow up. There are times when taking that quirky bend in the road is exactly right.

Well, here we are, in spitting distance of the year 2000. In some ways the world is changing at a dizzying pace. It is almost as if the excitement of the coming twenty-first century demands all kinds of new ways to speak, travel, work, and play. Already we study, communicate, learn, and work in ways that weren't possible just six or seven years ago—or even yesterday. People are using terms such as "the information superhighway," "surfing the Internet," and "the Web." Words such as "virtual reality" and "cyberspace" roll off the tongues of seven-year-olds who have to explain them to their parents. These were not part of our ordinary vocabulary a couple of years ago. The truth is that computers have revolutionized the way our teachers teach and students study and learn. The answer to just how much computers have changed the way education is being "delivered" (yes, there are people who actually believe education is something to deliver—like ice cream!) is still being assessed. Indeed, not all the questions have been asked, even though colleges and universities are rushing to adapt their campuses to the new technologies needed for distance learning. Professors are urged to develop new courses to be offered on the Web, or to teach a course at one college while students from another sit in front of a TV screen and interact with the professor and other students in the actual classroom. It may take years before students and professors can honestly evaluate a "virtual college education" as compared to a traditional one where professors and students are on a real college campus in a real classroom, discussing course material face-to-face. (However, just how much our world depends upon the new technology becomes abundantly clear each time we have a disastrous power failure, such as the one that brought life in San Francisco to a sudden halt on December 8, 1998.)

Just a few years ago most students who applied to colleges did so by sending for college catalogs and applying to anywhere from one to five or six colleges and universities, one-by-one. Today you can quickly check out twenty or thirty college catalogs sitting in your room with your computer, or if you don't have one, using the computer in your high school or public library. Professor Diane Gayeski, of the Park School of Communications at Ithaca College (Ithaca, New York) says, "a student who just relies on the catalog through the mail will be missing out, and will only be getting the older, typical experience. Computer technology gives a more in-depth and credible picture of who the alumni are and who the professors are and what they have published."

And, Linda Miller, Associate Dean of Admissions at the University of Virginia at Charlottesville, looks forward to the day when "all applications can be done through computers. It will be a lot less expensive because mailing is a huge problem and very expensive. We get 17,000 applicants, (although) we mail out 40,000-plus applications. To have our catalog and course offerings on the Web is a huge savings, not only for the university, but also for the applicant. A prospective student can ask questions and get answers far more easily on the Web than if they wrote letters. Kids now have instant access to the colleges."

But even without access to computers, you don't have to be afraid that the traditional method of applying to college will go away. "It is important," says Miller, "that we have all methods of applying available."

Because new technology seems to be forcing us to make changes in all areas of our lives, I think it's time for another look at what kinds of choices are out there for you and what kinds of skills you will need to succeed in this new Information Age. Actually it's still the same old world as before—only enhanced by a lot of great gadgets that even the most bumbling among us will eventually be called upon to use.

Yours will be the first generation to spend its entire adult life in the twenty-first century. Older folks, who remember being thrilled with electric typewriters, are all thumbs now that they have to grapple with this new technology and its tongue-twisting vocabulary. (I even remember the excitement over ballpoint pens versus ink pens. No, I never did write with a quill, but I do have a great artist friend who loves working with special inks and a sharpened turkey feather. He turns out exquisite works of art that simply can't ever be duplicated by a computer, although the computer can produce some very attractive art, too.)

What's exciting for you is that you already possess some of the greatest assets for success in the twenty-first century:

1. You are young and enthusiastic.

2. You have the ability to absorb all this new technology easily because you don't have to unlearn the old ways of communicating and working.

3. You are full of new and fresh ideas, and you understand how to make this new technology work for you. You can run Spell Check to catch your spelling errors, use a talking computer or Braille computer if you are blind, and employ a computer note pad to turn your handwritten scribbles into typed notes, to help you study— and so much more.

Today, business leaders and college presidents talk about the next stage of computers that will make communicating through the Web, Internet, or interactive television as easy and inexpensive as talking on the phone or turning on the radio. We're not there yet, but we are rapidly moving in that direction. Although we don't have to worry that the traditional college campuses will become obsolete, what we will see is that the world has become a much smaller place thanks to the rapid expansion of technology.

HUMAN BEINGS HAVEN'T CHANGED

No matter how fast technology changes the way we work and learn, we mere human beings don't change much at all. We still start out as infants, grow into little kids, make it to high school—and we still have to figure out what to do with our lives. In the nineteenth century, people didn't have a choice about the kind of work they did. A man did what his father did, and if you were a woman, you married someone your father chose for you and lived a life much the same as your mother's. The Industrial Revolution in the twentieth century moved us into the cities, where people began to exercise more choices.

ENDLESS CHOICES

As the twentieth century ends and the twenty-first begins, the concept of work is changing again. Men and women in the Information Age can expect to change jobs every few years. Many of you already have seen one or both parents change jobs several times—all too often laid off from a job at a company they believed would employ them until retirement.

You will probably change your job as many as six or seven times, and you may also totally change careers. You will find work and leisure activities that use a whole range of your talents. And instead of feeling as if your formal education is over once you graduate from college or other postsecondary training, you will need to think of yourself as a lifelong learner—one who continually looks for opportunities to update skills and acquire new information. Becoming an educated and employable person takes on a whole new meaning in the Information Age.

No matter how much the world changes, you are concerned right now with finding answers to the same important questions teenagers have been asking since the beginning of time:

Who am I?

Why am I here on this planet?

What am I supposed to do with my life?

Will I find someone to love, and will he/she love me back?

Am I going to be able to find work that means something more than just a paycheck?

Can I support myself?

Am I smart enough, good looking enough, tall/short enough?

Will I find friends?

What are my choices?

Do I have to follow in someone else's footsteps?

Do I really have to grow up?

These are the really important questions, and each of us must find the answers in our own way and in our own time. The people you will meet in this book grappled with these issues, too. Some, like Doug Leonard, reached a point where school was seen as boring and useless. Doug wanted to quit and get a job. He knew he would go to college at some point, but he said, "I needed to find out who I was."

Others were more like Lorin Dytel, who had gotten everything she could out of high school by the time she finished her sophomore year.

She was ready for college just after her sixteenth birthday. To win support for her desire to go to college early, Lorin had to battle not her parents, but her high school teachers and guidance counselors.

Nate Kipp, on the other hand, dutifully went off to college after high school without a clue as to what he wanted to do. After a painful year in which he found out he wasn't ready for college, he decided to take time out. Nate heard about AmeriCorps and took two years to do some serious community service with Habitat for Humanity.

Dan Elsberg honed his Spanish language skills by volunteering for two summers with Amigos de las Americas, a group that promotes good health in South American countries by sending in teams of young people to inoculate children against polio, measles, and other devastating childhood diseases. He did this while he was still in high school—and came to understand, appreciate, and value people from a different culture.

Each of these students, as well as others you will meet in this book, felt like square pegs in round holes for a while. But instead of trying to fit in where they didn't belong or didn't want to be, these students struck out on their own. All have taken risks, done the unexpected... and survived. In fact, many have become solid citizens their parents are proud of. Not surprisingly, others needed to take more time to figure out their lives and are still searching. Most importantly, the things they did helped them develop the confidence to tackle new situations and fearlessly break away from the pack. You will meet kids in this book who learned how to think through their options and make decisions. They learned how to argue constructively with their parents and guidance counselors—even their friends. They learned how to relate to and work with people who were vastly different from themselves. And each learned how to manage his or her time. Curiously enough, they developed the skills the experts tell us successful people will need in the unpredictable future.

Not everything they tried was an unqualified success. Sometimes a coveted job, internship, or community service project turned out to be awful. Michael Urgo thought he was going to land a great job in a ski town in British Columbia, only to find out the job didn't exist—and as a U.S. citizen, he wasn't able to get a work visa. More than one person went to college as an early admission student, only to feel over-whelmed by the challenge and doubtful about the choice. More often than not, the fear of failure and the possibility of someone saying "I knew it wouldn't work" was enough to keep a person going until things improved.

Even seemingly unhappy experiences had their own peculiar set of rewards. The old saying, "if all you have are lemons, make lemonade," applied in some tough situations. If there is a common thread that runs through all of the interviews, it is that by maintaining a tremendous spirit of adventure and moving out in new directions, kids, many just like you, felt they were in control of their lives. Even adversity has its rewards.

I hope this book will help in your choice of the "next step." Maybe you will decide that doubts about going to college right after high school are unfounded, and you are just going through the normal jitters before a new event. That's terrific. For you, sticking to the traditional path is the right choice.

But perhaps you will encounter people and ideas in this book that will make you think, "Hey! That's just the way I see things. If some-one else did that, so can I." That's just great. You will have made the right decision, too.

The truth is there is no one right way to grow up. And there is no way anyone can predict what the future holds for you. We are expe-riencing some of the most dramatic changes in this world since the Industrial Revolution. You are lucky to be in on the cutting edge of the most exciting century ever. But you have to be prepared to try more things and take more risks than others who have come before you. Don't fret over little mistakes. They help you grow. Learn to listen to that inner voice that is always with you. If you think you are doing what's best for you, you probably are. Conversely, if your heart quickens because what you are about to do seems wrong, step back and take a long, hard look at what you've chosen. You may want to change directions.

You can't stop change from happening any more than you can stop yourself from growing up. (That is, in fact, the answer to the question, "Do I have to grow up?")

The best of luck in whatever you choose. And remember, plan to have a lot of fun along the way.

Chapter I

Who Am I? Why Am I On This Planet?

RIGHT NOW YOU ARE SUPPOSED TO BE HAVING THE TIME OF YOUR LIFE. Isn't that what all the adults are telling you? After all, besides being in the bloom of youth, you are coming of age during the dawn of a new century— the Information Age. (Virtually anyone who was your age at the turn of the last century is long dead, but they must have felt the excitement you are feeling now.) All kinds of new possibilities will be open to you—so many, in fact, it's hard to figure out where to begin.

Are you someone who thinks that if only you could figure out what you want to do, you'd go ahead and do it? Or, do you know exactly what you want but feel as if you are drowning in a sea of boredom? If the good fairy could grant you one wish, would it be that you would be some place where you are intellectually challenged—some place where other kids would know what you are talking about? Or better yet, understand your jokes?

Ever since junior high school, teachers and parents have been exhorting you to plan for your future. But how can you plan for the future if you haven't a clue about what you want or can do? How can you find out what's out there in the world for you? How do people figure out their life's work, anyway? And will you have to do the same work your whole life?

Sometimes it's hard enough to plan what to do on Saturday night, let alone for the rest of your life. Other times it's easier to sketch out the big picture, but it's impossible to decide which college you might want to attend, which subjects you'd like to study, or even if now is the right time to go to college. Or you may be thinking, "Do I really have to go to college at all, when all I want to do is travel . . . or get a job so I can finally earn some money and be on my own?" Or, "Why can't I go to college right now since there isn't anything left for me to take in high school?"

And then there is the enormous sum of money you hear that college costs these days. Somehow the idea of being deep in debt at age twenty-two isn't exactly what you had in mind as a way to begin your adult working life. And sticking your parents with your college debt, when they might have other kids to put through college, could put them in hock for the rest of their lives! Yet, if you don't go to college, or get postsecondary education of some sort, your chances of earning a good living in the Information Age are pretty slim.

What do people mean when they say these are the best years of your life? The most confusing years are more like it.

Your parents tell you that you have to go to college, but it will probably bankrupt them.

Your teachers tell you that without an education you'll never earn enough money to support yourself.

Your music tells you that the most important thing in life is falling in love.

Your friends tell you to live for the moment.

And inside of you a small voice is saying, "Hey! Stop the world. I want to get off."

Don't panic.

Other kids have felt the way you do right now. (In fact, so did your parents and teachers when they were your age.) Most of us manage to grow up and find work we love or at least like. The journey may seem hit or miss, but every time you try something new, you add to your store of life skills.

Now is the time to investigate a whole range of options before deciding what to do after high school. You might travel to a foreign country where you can meet people and learn a new language, do a summer internship in a field that interests you, work with a disadvantaged population, gain solid work skills and earn money toward your college education, volunteer for a non profit organization, or test yourself in an Outward Bound program. If you are willing to try some things that are off the beaten path, you will have the opportunity to grow in ways you never thought possible.

Chris Batt, from Wilmington, Delaware, dutifully went off to college after he finished high school but really couldn't figure out why he was there. He decided to work for a while in a sporting goods store. In his spare time he coached crew (rowing) with inner-city youth. In the back of his mind, he dreamed of a career in television. When a college counselor suggested he take part in an internship program called Dynamy, Inc., in Worcester, Massachusetts, Chris got a chance to work at channel WGMC, where he and other interns got to "do everything." Chris learned that internships are invaluable in helping a person figure out the "next step."

The day Lucy Morris's grandmother took her to Sugarbush airport near Montpelier, Vermont, when she was 14, Lucy knew she wanted to fly. She fulfilled that dream at 18. Then she had to figure out how she could earn a living flying. Later, with her college degree in flight management, Lucy found flight instructor opportunities somewhat limited. But today, at 24, she is looking forward to a hitch with the Coast Guard, hoping that she will be given the kind of responsibility she craves.

"With my flight management degree, the Coast Guard will probably give me more responsibility sooner than, say, some of the 18-year-olds who joined up when I did. I don't know what's in store for me, but I'm excited," she said when she'd finished her basic training and was waiting for her first ship assignment.

William Glass lived in a small village in upstate New York and had taken all of the advanced placement math and science courses offered at his high school by the time he was finished with his freshman year. He knew he was ready for college. "But I didn't want to go to a university, where I'd just be mixed in with everybody else," he says. He applied to and was accepted at The Clarkson School in Potsdam, New York. Clarkson provided Will with a one-year "bridge" program. He lived and studied with other students like himself in a dorm set aside for them on the Clarkson campus. He took regular classes at Clarkson University. At the end of the year, he had a year's worth of valuable college credits and was ready to transfer to M.I.T. The Clarkson School was, Will says, "the first real academic challenge I'd had."

John Weeldreyer of Chapel Hill, North Carolina, just couldn't figure out what it was he wanted to do after high school, but he knew he needed to get himself organized. "I didn't want to go to college. I didn't have money or parental support at that time." He checked out the possibilities in the armed forces and decided to join the Navy for two years. "It was the best thing I ever did for myself," John says.

"I wanted some time away from my family so that I could grow up."

Chris Biacioni of Ithaca, New York, had studied Spanish for all four years of high school, but wanted to be totally fluent before she went off to college. "And," she says, "I wanted some time away from my family so that I could grow up. I want to feel as though I can take care of myself." She applied to her local Rotary International club to spend a year in Mexico. Chris's family hosted a Rotary student from the Netherlands during her senior year, and they became great friends. Now Chris looks forward to living with a Mexican family. It doesn't matter to her that most of her friends will be going off to college or that she'll be doing an extra year of high school in a foreign language and in another country. This will be a year for her to fulfill one of her dreams.

How are you going to figure out if you're the kind of person who will be making the right choice if you do the traditional thing: high school, college, career, and maybe graduate or professional school sandwiched in there somewhere?

How will you know if you decide to go to college a year or two early that you won't be giving up the best part of high school and growing up too fast—or worse yet, that you aren't really emotionally ready to accept the challenge of college?

If you decide to postpone college for a couple of years, or stop out after a year or so into college, how can you know that you will return to complete your education? Maybe after a year or more away from the books, you won't remember how to study—or want to. And if you do put off college for a year or two, won't you feel that you are too old to be just starting college? What will happen if you decide to stop out for work or travel, and you can't find a job or your travel plans fall through? Or maybe college isn't really important at all. It's all so confusing—isn't there someplace to get some facts?

WHERE TO GET RELIABLE INFORMATION

The U.S. Department of Labor tracks the employment and earning possibilities for high school graduates compared with college graduates. Three things stand out:

First, the more you learn, the more you earn. For the year 1995 (the last year the survey was done in New York state), the median wage for high school graduates aged twenty-five to thirty-four was $27,100; for college graduates in the same age bracket, the median wage climbed to $42,700. That's a whopping $15,600 difference. Just ten years earlier, the earning gap between high school and college graduates was only $9,000 and ten years before that, just $4,000. You don't need to be a math whiz to see in which direction this is going.

Second, the unemployment rates are equally impressive: fewer than three percent of the college graduates in that age group are unemployed. With some college, the unemployment rate is between four and five percent. A high school graduate's chance of being unemployed jumps to nearly eight percent, and for those without a high school diploma, the unemployment rate is eleven percent.

Third, there's more bad news for people without a college education. The number of jobs that don't require a college diploma is shrinking—even jobs that formerly required no more than a high school diploma now want workers with some college training. Many factory jobs that used to pay good wages are either in decline or being moved to foreign countries, where there is a ready supply of cheaper labor.

WHAT SKILLS WILL YOU NEED?

Peter Francese, founder of *American Demographics Magazine,* which is read by people who work in government, business, and academia all over the English-speaking world, carefully studies the reports put out by the Labor Department and other government agencies. As the title of this magazine suggests, Mr. Francese is especially interested in population figures and reports on how shifting populations influence the job market. He and his editors use the information gained from a variety of government sources to make predictions about job growth and decline in specific areas. Mr. Francese is able to identify the skills needed to succeed in this global information-hungry age.

"The first of these," he says, "is the ability to write very well." There are many different kinds of writing skills, he notes. One kind of writing is to be able to look at a set of facts and describe them. "But the ability to look at a set of facts and tell a story . . . is an enormously valuable skill . . . that kind of skill takes years to learn, and it is not something that is right or wrong. It is a skill which is continually updated."

The second is "the ability to communicate verbally with people, to be persuasive, and to be convincing in terms of your point of view. So much of what is done in business and education and health care today is done in meetings, and is done with people who . . . pool their knowledge and use the combined information to solve a problem."

One skill everyone should have, no matter what you do, says Mr. Francese, is typing. He also recommends that you learn a second language. "It almost doesn't matter which language, but my personal preference is Spanish. But people who can write and speak Chinese or Japanese are just immensely in demand. Such a person can make anywhere from 50 to 100 percent more on a regular basis than a person who speaks only one language."

Learn how to manage yourself! "The ability to make intelligent choices about how to spend one's time, and (know) what sorts of activities are going to be beneficial . . . will keep you healthy and competitive with others."

And finally, Mr. Francese says it's important to learn how to manage others. "People who can manage human resources (other people) are more valuable than people who can't."

WHERE ARE THE JOBS?

Based on the U.S. Department of Labor and other sources, Mr. Francese identifies three major areas with enormous growth and a variety of job opportunities within each field. These are health care, education, and information services.

1. Health care, Mr. Francese notes, is "a trillion dollar industry." He points out that our population is aging in a very specific manner. "In the next decade the fastest growing age group will be people in their fifties. And around the age of 50 people begin to become afflicted with chronic things like diabetes, high blood pressure, and other such things, as well as general wear and tear on the body." There are literally tens of millions of aging "baby boomers," and they will need all kinds of medical attention and a variety of traditional and non-traditional therapies.

In addition to the aging boomers, people over 85 will number between three and five million. They will require home health care and care in a variety of nursing home facilities.

Of course, as we move into the second decade of the twenty-first century, there will be another population shift. Health care will continue to be a growing industry, not just in providing care but also in the area of providing information and record keeping, as well as in basic scientific research.

2. Education is the second growth industry. Mr. Francese finds that there will be a "clump" of teens moving into the late teen and early adult bracket. There will be a 16 percent growth in this age group— from 25 million to 29 million. The demand for teachers at all levels will increase, as will the demand for people who can create educational materials, including educational software, CD-ROMs, and other materials that help people learn in "a computerized environment."

3. Information processing is the third area of growth. "There is," says Mr. Francese, "an absolute explosion in the number of firms that provide geographic data," as well as environmental data, consumer information, and natural resource management, among other areas. "There are immense opportunities in the area of information processing . . . and any young person who has the natural facility for analysis of numerical information has a very bright future."

ALL THERE IS, IS CHANGE. NO CHANGE—NO LIFE!

Whether we realize it or not, we all build on the skills we already have. Even if you think you don't know very much right now, you know more than you think. You may be great in math, computers, or music. You may excel in language or in simply getting people to cooperate with each other. You may already have a burning interest in politics or biology or bicycles or earthworms. Or you may be a science fiction buff or someone who held a part-time job after school at a tofu factory. The idea is that there are things you already know, and things you may want to learn later, and things you haven't yet thought about learning.

In this great new Information Age you will be expected to accept change, to try new things and adapt to new situations. Whether you feel excited, terrified, or indifferent about change doesn't matter. Knowing yourself, your talents and capabilities, will help you move on. And although you "may not

"Knowing yourself, your talents and capabilities, will help you move on."

be sure of what it is you want to do, or even what's out there for you, it's important to keep your options open," says Dr. George Conneman, retired director of instruction at the College of Agriculture and Life Sciences at Cornell University.

There's no better time than right now to start thinking about what's special about yourself.

KNOW THYSELF

Here is a test you may want to try. Actually, it isn't really a test. It's a tool to help you create a picture of yourself. There are no wrong or right answers to any of the questions. And there are no "trick" questions. Since you don't keep score, you can't flunk. But do make the answers your own rather than what you think somebody else thinks you should be doing.

This isn't even one of those tests that is supposed to tell you what you should be when you grow up. What you may get, however, are some clues about the direction you can take over the next couple of years.

The items on the test represent a variety of skills, attitudes, personal qualities, information, and understandings you may or may not have—and you may or may not want to have. All the items included here have been found at some time, in some place, to be valuable in the

"There's no better time than right now to start thinking about what's special about yourself."

adult world. No one, regardless of age or achievement, would be likely to rank at the high end for all the items.

You are invited to think about your skills and your personal development. Consider what you believe you are good at, and think about whether or not you want to put your energy into improving in some weak areas over the next year or so or in using your strengths in a new way.

The idea for this self-assessment test came from Joan Webster who for many years taught and counseled men and women at Vermont College. She developed this test for people who were starting college as older students. Many of them had been housewives and mothers. Others had worked in factories and on farms. Most were unsure of their skills and had doubts about their ability to perform in a college setting. Ms. Webster found that this kind of test helped them sort things out. Together, Ms. Webster and I revised the test so that it can help you think through your own development as a young person on the brink of adulthood.

You may want to assess yourself more than once. It's a good idea to make several copies of the test before marking it up. If you copy it on different colored paper, it may help when you go back and check yourself out.

Try the test now, and after you've had a chance to think about it, put it away in a drawer. In a couple of months, after you've made some decisions about your future plans and have been engaged in them for a while, take the test again. You will be amazed at how many new skills you've acquired and how many of your attitudes have changed. Study the results carefully.

"You may want to assess yourself more than once."

They will help you create a picture of yourself that will move you on into the adult world.

Of course, there are many other kinds of aptitude tests given by educational professionals. A good test may help you sort out what professions might be right for you. Many tests are based on the special interests and skills of successful lawyers, teachers, scientists, etc. The theory is that certain people with the same personality traits tend to do well in certain careers.

"No one test, however, can hold all the answers for you. You need to follow what is in your heart."

However, even if it turns out that you share the same traits as successful surgeons, if you can't stand the sight of blood, you'd probably do well to stay away from surgery, but you might consider other careers in the medical field.

There are many tests geared to helping you define your choices. The Strong-Campbell Inventory Test measures your interests against 100 people who are happy and successful in a variety of careers. There's SIGI, a computerized values clarification test, the Jackson Vocational Interest Survey, and the Kuder Preference Record, which measures occupational interests, to name just a few. Your high school guidance counselor, an educational consultant, or college career officer can tell you where you can take these tests if you are interested in finding out more. No one test, however, can hold all the answers for you. You need to follow what is in your heart.

SELF-ASSESSMENT

Name [   ]   **Date** [   ]

For each item, show your judgment of yourself by filling in spaces to create a bar. You may stop at any bar anywhere between high and low.

LOW   **HIGH**

Writing ability

For example, for the skill "Writing Ability," here's how you might fill in the boxes:

LOW   **HIGH**

Writing ability

"Writing is something I don't do well."

OR...

Writing ability

"My writing isn't horrible, but it isn't great."

OR...

Writing ability

"My writing ability is alright but could be better."

OR...

Writing ability

"Writing is something I do very well."

PART I:
GENERAL ACADEMIC SKILLS

	LOW	HIGH
Writing ability		
Reading comprehension		
Ability to express ideas orally		
Ability to understand what others say		
Ability to ask questions		
Ability to seek and try solutions to problems		
Ability to solve complex mathematical problems		
Ability to do everyday mathematical problems		
Ability to concentrate on difficult reading material		
Ability to formulate questions		
Ability to seek out teachers and other experts to help clarify difficult material		
Ability to work independently in library		
Ability to study with other students		
Ability to study different material alone		
Ability to complete school work on time		
Ability to complete assignments in subjects that are least liked		
Ability to become absorbed in a new subject		
Ability to share ideas with classmates		

PART II:
PERSONAL AND INTERPERSONAL
ATTITUDES AND QUALITIES

Personal:	LOW		HIGH

Self-confidence

Physical fitness

Ability to set short-range personal goals

List three short-range goals, if possible:

1.

2.

3.

Ability to set long-range personal goals

List three long-range goals, if possible:

1.

2.

3.

Tolerance for frustration

Development of a personal value system

Indicate what you value most, if possible:

1.

2.

3.

Ability to finish projects you initiate

Ability to work without supervision

Ability to be alone

Willingness to try something physically demanding

Willingness to change plans for a new challenge

LOW   HIGH

Willingness to
learn new tasks

Ability to take criticism

Willingness to take
acalculated risk

Ability to receive
compliments

Willingness to
be innovative

Willingness to
challenge yourself

Ability to act on intuition

Ability to appreciate
your own strengths

Ability to like yourself

Ability to bounce back
after you have been
criticized

Ability to laugh at yourself

Ability to make
use of leisure time

Ability to develop
new hobbies

INTERPERSONAL

Ability to work with peers

Ability to work
with older people

Ability to adapt to
new situations

Ability to get along with
different kinds of people
who are of the same age

Ability to get along
with older people

Ability to "fit in" with
new social situations

LOW   **HIGH**

Willingness to take
"orders" from someone
who may not be as
smart as you

Ability to do a boring or
unpleasant task for pay

Willingness to
learn new tasks

Ability to make
the best of things

Willingness to stick to
your guns when you're
convinced you're right

INFORMATION & SKILLS

Acquisition of specific
information or skill

Name your special interests:

1.

2.

3.

INFORMATION

Knowledge of how city and
county government works

Knowledge of how
state government works

Knowledge of local issues

Name specific issues of concern:

1.

2.

3.

Knowledge of
national affairs

Name specific issues of concern:

1.

2.

3.

LOW   HIGH

Knowledge of world affairs

Name specific issues of concern:

1.

2.

3.

Knowledge of history

1. world

2. national

3. state

4. local

Understanding of
others' cultures

Specify, if possible:

1.

2.

3.

Understanding of how
people behave and why

Knowledge of the sciences

Name areas, if possible:

1.

2.

3.

Exploring the arts (art,
music, drama, dance)

Name activities and forms:

1.

2.

3.

Knowledge of mathematics

Understanding of
your own past

Knowledge of where
different countries are
located on a world map

	LOW	HIGH
Knowledge of the geography of the United States		
Knowledge of computers:		
word processing		
programming		
computer language		

SKILLS

Skill in reading and understanding maps

Skill in working with hands

Specific areas:

1.

2.

3.

Skill in working with complex machines

Specific machines:

1.

2.

3.

PART II: PERSONAL AND INTERPERSONAL

1. What are the qualities and attitudes I identified as strongest in part I?

2. Of these, which do I want to develop further?

3. Which things do I want to work on now, and which do I want to set aside for "someday"?

4. Which attitudes and qualities do I think will help me in planning my next step?

5. Of those areas which I want to develop further, which are for "someday" and which are for "now"?

When you have done more than one self-assessment, place the last two next to each other and ask yourself about the changes you see in your responses. Ask yourself, "How do I explain each difference? Was each the result of a plan or did it just happen? What do I want to do next? What should I shelve for a later time?"

Take time to appreciate yourself before deciding what to do next, whether you are doing the assessment for the first time or comparing versions. The good thing is you don't need to learn everything at once. You've got a whole lifetime ahead of you, and you will be learning all the time.

In the following chapters you will read about people your age who made choices about their immediate future that didn't exactly match what their friends were doing. As you read about what they did and how they did it, you may want to think how they would have responded to the self-assessment test you've just completed. And you may want to consider how you might feel attempting something a little off the beaten track.

Chapter II

Stopping Out: Is It Right For You?

SHOULD YOU PUT YOUR COLLEGE EDUCATION ON HOLD? For some, the answer may be a resounding "yes." You may not, for example, be a particularly good student in high school. Do your teachers write "does not live up to his/her potential" on your report card? Do you know you really could do A or B work if you actually did some studying? Do you feel you will be wasting your time if you go to college now? Or, are you suffering from senior burnout and needing to relax and think about your goals for a while? Do you simply not have the money to pay for the college you really want to attend? Working and saving your money for a year or two could certainly help. Perhaps there are some things you'd like to do now, while you are young and without responsibilities—travel, community service, living in a foreign country, etc. The diverse reasons for stopping out, as you will see from the stories here, may strike a chord with you.

It's easy to make your friends believe that striking out in a direction different from what your parents expect is a sensible and sane idea. Convincing your parents and even your guidance counselor (to say nothing of your Uncle Manny, a nice guy who has been stuck in a dead-end job because he dropped out of high school years ago, and who thinks you'll wind up like him) may take some doing.

Deans of admissions at prestigious colleges and universities are generally enthusiastic about students who take time out between high school and college.

"It's a fine thing to do, and we will defer a student for a year," says Linda Miller, associate dean of admissions at the University of Virginia in Charlottesville. "However, we ask that the student submit a plan on how they expect to find themselves in some way. We want them to do something in a constructive way for a while."

Who Stops Out?

- Those who need to raise money for college.
- Students who take themselves seriously and are self-directed.
- Students who have no real reason for being in college.
- Independent-minded students who are not overly influenced by their peers.
- Students for whom an unusual opportunity presents itself.
- Outgoing, high achievers who are risk-takers.
- Students who have spent a year or two in college and need a break from academic life.
- Students who need to prove to themselves that they can be independent.

Yet there are compelling arguments for going directly to college after high school:

Going to college right after high school is the normal and traditional thing to do.

Going to college right away allows a person to make realistic career plans.

Entering college right after high school maintains the momentum of study habits.

It is easier to make friends during freshman year when everybody is roughly the same age.

Students who want to take a year out to work or study abroad or do an internship are more likely to be accepted to the competitive programs if they already have some college years behind them.

PARENTS NEED TO BE CONVINCED

If you can step away from yourself and your own problems for a moment and think about why your parents might not agree with your decision, you may be able to prove to your parents that you are mature enough to make this kind of decision. (Shouting, "I'm 18 (or 16 or 17). I'm old enough to make my own decisions," generally doesn't do much to prove your maturity.) Once you understand their concerns, you have a much better chance of marshaling your arguments and gaining parental approval. The more information you have before you bring up your plans, the better you'll be able to argue your case successfully. Not surprisingly, once parents understand that what you are doing is a positive action and not a negative one, they may even be pleased with your decision—or at least accept it.

WHO STOPS OUT AND WHY

Dissatisfied With School

Alice Saul didn't like high school. "By the end of it I was ready to leave everything," she says. "I didn't have much fun there even though I was a cheerleader. I wasn't with people I wanted to be with. I definitely wanted to be someplace else." In fact, by graduation Alice wasn't particularly motivated to think much about her future at all. Finally, it was Alice's mom who made a suggestion: (Contrary to what you may have thought, moms, dads, and even teachers often do make excellent suggestions now and then.)

"How about living in a foreign country for a while?"

Now that idea appealed to Alice.

"My mother's only requirement was that I had to be in a program. I couldn't just hop on a plane and travel around by myself." Her mother suggested that Alice research programs in Europe, while she offered to get some information on programs in Israel.

"So of course I didn't do anything," Alice admits. And when the brochures describing a variety of opportunities for young people in Israel came through the mail slot, Alice said, "OK, I guess I'll go to Israel." Even though Alice and her mom are Jewish and celebrated many of the traditional Jewish holidays, they didn't belong to a temple or synagogue.

What Your Parents Might Say

- *You will be wasting time.*
- *Everybody else is going to college, and you will lose all your friends.*
- *You may never go to college if you stop out.*
- *You won't learn anything of value by stopping out.*
- *You are too young to make that kind of decision.*
- *It will be too difficult to study after you've been away from school.*
- *Once you get to college you'll be glad that you listened to us.*
- *It's always been our dream to send you to college.*
- *If you stop out you will lose your scholarship.*
- *Don't even think it. You're going to college and that's that.*

Alice found herself suddenly excited to learn more about her Jewish roots.

I Was the Bad Kid

Michael Urgo says, "I wasn't sure where I wanted to be and what I wanted to do. My freshman and sophomore year in high school were spent in (Washington) DC, and I did miserably in school. I was kind of a bad kid and got sent to boarding school. I come from a family of 10 children, nine boys and one girl. And I was the only one sent away. I have four older brothers and they are all successful. And then there was me."

Even though Michael did all right at boarding school, he just couldn't decide on a college. "The applications would scare me. I didn't want to do it. I didn't want to go to school." Nevertheless, he wound up at a small all-male southern college because he was offered a sports scholarship. "But there wasn't much to do there except drugs. So I got into that and I failed out of school and came back home." After going "through the motions" again at a local community college, Michael realized he was just wasting his time. And he wanted to get away.

"I knew I wanted to be on the West Coast," he says. So he tried to get a job in British Columbia through "something called Interwest." But when he arrived in Canada, Michael discovered the job didn't exist. "I was 19, and I didn't have a job and I didn't want to leave. So I worked under the table. I'd save some money, and then I'd go rock climbing or kayaking or skiing. I was living an incredible life." But after six months

"I wasn't sure where I wanted to be and what I wanted to do."

Michael knew he was just being irresponsible, and at his parents' insistence, he came back home. Still, Michael felt his time in British Columbia was important in terms of becoming "closer to the outdoors, and a kind of spirituality."

I Wanted to Live in a Warm Climate

Nora Schmidt was accepted at five of the six colleges she applied to, but one day woke up feeling "I didn't want to do that. I wasn't ready for college. I wanted to live independently. This was always an issue for me. I always wanted to do my thing, and my parents wanted me to do their thing." Nora had visited the Virgin Islands during a school trip, and decided that she would move there for four months. And "instead of four months, it turned out to be four years!" Nora secured her first job at some campgrounds that offered room (in a tent) and board in exchange for working 20 hours a week. Before she left, her parents handed her a "four page single-spaced list of reasons why I shouldn't go." One reason was that while they would promise her money towards her college education at that time, they couldn't promise that money would be there at a later date. And "if I didn't get a college education, I wouldn't get anywhere in the world." Unfazed, Nora left for the Virgin Islands anyway.

"I didn't want to do that. I wasn't ready for college."

Nora's job at the campgrounds lasted for about a year. Her second job was on another part of the island—waitressing in a vegetarian restaurant. But a collision between her first car, just 24 hours after she bought it, and a Mack truck nearly cost her life, and put her on crutches for some time. And she had to find another job where she wouldn't be on her feet all day. Barely a week after Nora got off her crutches, "the hurricane hit, which just devastated the island. By all the rules of nature, I should have died in that," she says. Although people on the island didn't think this was going to be a major hurricane, the reality was quite different." What began as a Category 1 hurricane was quickly upgraded to Category 2 and then to Category 3. Then, "in a split second it was over us, and no one could leave. And then the radio went dead. You know, you just can't win over Mother Nature," says Nora, who says she found herself actually praying for her life as the walls in the small house she was living in came crashing down around her, and the muddy water poured in. Somehow Nora and her housemate managed to make it to a crawl space under the house, and after about seven hours, the wind finally died down and they were able to reach a house that somehow had remained untouched by the storm. For some reason, Nora says, she survived. "I was given another chance."

A Need To Save for College

Aaron Seymour from Pittsfield, Massachusetts, was "into doing things with nature." The first year he was out of high school he heard about AmeriCorps, a nationwide program initiated by President Clinton in 1994. It is a national service movement that gives young people who are eighteen years or older the opportunity to do community service for up to two years (or in some cases, three years) in exchange for a modest living stipend plus money to either help pay off existing college loans or to help finance college, graduate school, or vocational training. There are literally hundreds of programs to choose from in every region of the United States.

Aaron applied and was accepted to the Conservation Corps right in his own community. He worked a thirty-hour week and was paid $5.86 an hour. In addition, he received medical insurance and an education award of $4,725 for each year he successfully completed. And because Aaron was able to live at home, he saved a good part of his living stipend.

"We do things like brush cutting or helping the Massachusetts Audubon Society clean up the bird sanctuaries. We do painting and repairs to the senior citizens' home which is run by the Massachusetts Public Housing Authority. I've also done some public service announcements on radio and TV on composting and recycling toxic waste products, with advice on how to properly dispose of car batteries."

A Devastating Accident Didn't Put His Life on Hold

When Trampas Strucker woke up after surgery his family were all standing around his bed. They were crying. "My dad (who is a physician) was trying to tell me that I couldn't ever again use my legs. I looked at him and said, 'Quit whining about what I can't do. I want to start concentrating on what I can do.' That was the first sentence out of my mouth (since the accident)."

Right after an incredibly successful rodeo where Trampas, who had been riding professionally since age twelve, placed first in bare back riding in Vancouver, Canada, he and his riding partner drove back to Kasmir, Washington, where they met up with his partner's parents. "They were riding their Honda Goldman 1150, and we decided to switch and bring the bike home." With his partner in front, the two boys pulled out and had gone less than four tenths of a mile on the highway when the kickstand hit the pavement. Trampas was thrown over the guardrail. "I was traveling about

"Quit whining about what I can't do. I want to start concentrating on what I can do."

45 miles per hour, and I hit hard enough for my spine to come up through my body and hit my sternum in two places. I totally shattered two discs, had thirteen breaks in six ribs, plus multiple fractures in my right arm. And I stretched my spinal cord eight inches. When I first woke up I had minimal use of my arms and hand. Within four days (against all odds) I had total use of them."

When the doctors at the University of Washington hospital told Trampas it would be six to nine months before he could leave the rehabilitation center, he said, "No way. I told them I'd be out of there in two, and they told me 'no way.' Three weeks later the doctors let Trampas attend the biggest rodeo in the state. He had already done the equivalent of three and a half months of rehab work. "My doctor let me go home for the stampede, and then I went back, and four weeks later I got released permanently. And I went back to high school and graduated with my class."

Despite the fact that he will never have use of his legs again, Trampas insisted on getting back into virtually all of the physical activities he'd been doing before the accident. "You know, I have this attitude that when anybody says I can't, I just say, 'I gotta try.' They said I'd never ride horses again, but within two or three months I was riding horses every single day. And everybody said, 'oh, you can't snow ski, and I went ahead and now I snow ski. And a while ago, I wanted to get back to rock climbing, and everybody said, 'oh, you can't rock climb.' I've been rock climbing all summer, enjoying it as much as I did before. It's all upper body. Ropes and upper body. I climbed for seven

"You know, I have this attitude that when anybody says I can't, I just say, 'I gotta try.'"

or eight years before I got hurt, since I was about twelve. So I knew the fundamentals." He does allow as how it is a "bit more difficult to do it without your legs."

It was right after he came back from his first rock climbing experience after the accident that he learned about AmeriCorps. Teachers and friends had told him about an opening that would allow Trampas to work with kids in the Ponasket School District. "So," says Trampas, "I looked into it, got the paperwork done, and got the job."

The University of the Road

Sam Godin of Ithaca, New York, was a sophomore at the State University of New York at Binghamton when a friend from his high school days phoned.

"They needed a keyboard player for their band, The Tribulations, and I'd played with four of the guys since my junior year in high school." Sam also plays guitar, bass, and the melodica—a little wind instrument with a keyboard. After high school graduation, his musician friends went off to the Berklee School of Music in Boston. Sam headed for SUNY Binghamton, where he majored in film.

"But I was involved with music even though I was officially studying film," Sam says. "Music has always been my primary interest."

It didn't take Sam more than a couple of minutes to make up his mind to join the band, at least for the summer. "I literally packed my bags in Binghamton right after my last exam and was in Boston that night to work with the band. We were performing within a week."

There were eleven guys in all (one was a full-time sound engineer and

> "We were performing within a week."

the other was a merchandise salesman), who, along with the band's gear, had to fit into a 15-person van.

"It was a great summer," Sam recalls, "much better than I had expected. I was becoming tighter with the band musically and socially, and we were writing a lot of new material."

By the end of the summer, August 1992, the band arrived in Los Angeles, where they found they had made the semifinals of the National Yamaha Soundcheck competition. Out of 4,000 other U.S. bands, they had been chosen to compete against the top 40. You can imagine how astonished they were when they actually won the grand prize, which included an opportunity to represent the U.S. for MusicQuest '92 in Tsomogoi, Japan. Sam decided to leave school and stick with the band.

"My mom was all for it," he says. "My dad had some reservations." But the chance to "make it" in the tough music world was just too good an opportunity to ignore. They all believed it wouldn't be long before the major record companies would offer them a contract.

The Family Rebel

By the time Matt Thomas had graduated from high school, he'd been working full time for three years at a local restaurant. By his own admission, he was an extremely angry and rebellious teenager. At 14, he moved out of his mom's house to live with his dad. When that didn't work out, he moved out and tried to make it on his own. He cut school more often than not and soon wound up in trouble with the authorities after he and a friend were caught trying to break into a private home. A month's incarceration in a juvenile detention center helped Matt understand that he had to stop lying, both to himself and others, in order to turn his life around. Then, with his parents' approval, he lived on his own, while working and going to school.

"I was eager to grow up," he admits. "I wanted to prove I could support myself." Matt managed to graduate with a New York State Regents high school diploma at the same time he worked full time in a restaurant.

For a while he flirted with the idea of enrolling in one of the prestigious culinary schools, but "I wasn't ready to take any kind of school seriously. I wanted hands-on experience in the restaurant business."

At 18 Matt had become the number two person in the best French restaurant in town.

"Both the head chef and sous chef had quit in the same week, just seven months after I started working in this place," says Matt, "and the owner hired a head chef and promoted me. I got a crash course in 'line cooking.'" But soon after his promotion, the restaurant burned down. Matt found other work until the restaurant was rebuilt. It reopened as a steak house, and Matt has been the sous chef ever since.

Two years have passed, and Matt has begun to give his future some serious thought. He realizes the only advancement he can make is as head chef, and that isn't likely. Also, standing on his feet for eight or ten hours a night has serious consequences. Matt has already had one operation on his knee.

Going to college to get an education looks much more attractive.

As a first step, Matt has decided to update his math skills at the local community college so he can take the SATs. He has found other courses that interest him and has made the decision to become a full-time student.

"I wanted to prove I could support myself."

"I'm ready to go back to school," he says. "But I'm not good enough yet for a four-year college, so I'm starting my education at the community college level, and I think I'm ready to work at my studies full time."

Matt's parents are delighted. They have offered to pay his college expenses so that he won't have to continue working full time. "I'm not sure I like the idea of them supporting me, but I also know that I won't be able to do justice to my studies if I continue to work at the pace I'm doing now.

"You know, I was so eager to grow up fast, but now . . . I wouldn't mind some play time." At this juncture, going to college will allow Matt to have some "play time" along with some serious academic work.

Not Mature Enough for College

Nate Kipp from Cleveland, Ohio, was a student at Ohio Wesleyan University. "But I wasn't mature enough for college, and after my first year I was looking for something else to do."

At his father's suggestion Nate attended a meeting of Habitat for Humanity, a program that helps people, who can't otherwise own a home, build affordable houses with volunteer labor and donated materials. Former United States President Jimmy Carter and his wife, Rosalynn, are major supporters of Habitat and often take up a hammer and saw to work alongside other volunteers. Generally, people do not get paid for volunteering for this organization, but it is now part of AmeriCorps

"You know, I was so eager to grow up fast, but now . . . I wouldn't mind some play time."

and offers the same opportunity for qualified students as other AmeriCorps projects.

"It seemed like a pretty good thing," says Nate. "The first year I was in Homestead, Florida, where we built houses for people who had lost homes in the hurricane. We started on Jordan Commons, a 200-home project. We had a lot to do and were kept very busy." In addition to the unpaid volunteers, there were between ten and 20 AmeriCorps people on the site.

A Plan to Volunteer in an African Nation

Sue Schwartz has always been active in her church and was a solid B student all through high school. She decided not to apply to college right away. What she wanted to do was to volunteer in Zimbabwe. "I had read *Cry, The Beloved Country*" (a classic novel by Alan Paton about racial inequality and injustice in South Africa)," she says, and it moved her. So Sue researched various organizations that have volunteers in Third World countries. She mailed dozens of applications. "I was really into saving the world," says Sue. "I wanted to check out the real world before going to college."

"I wanted to check out the real world before going to college."

To Sue's dismay, she was rejected everywhere. No one seemed to want a high school graduate with few qualifications to volunteer in Africa.

She took a job at a local cafe and tried to save up some money while continuing her search. Finally she located a small nonprofit organization, Educate the Children, which runs education programs for poor children in Nepal. Two months later, Sue found herself in Katmandu, learning Nepali and teaching English in a small private school for lower caste children.

Time Out for Reflection

Leana Horowitz went to high school in Watkins Glen, New York. She'd spent her junior high school year as a Rotary exchange student in Japan. It was during this year abroad that her mother first suggested she consider taking a year off after completing high school to reflect upon her Japanese experience.

"We corresponded frequently during that year, and gradually the idea took hold." Her father "thought that if I took a year off, I'd never go to college. But in my mind, that was never a problem. I love school."

Leana was accepted to Harvard University. On the acceptance form there was a check-off for deferred admission. When Leana pointed this out to her dad, he relaxed a little. He realized that stopping out wasn't just a whim of Leana's. In fact, at some universities, as many as 10 percent of incoming freshmen opt to defer admission for a year or more. Once Leana was assured, in writing, that her financial aid package would not be changed (unless, of course, the family income changed), she checked off the deferred admission box. Then she set about looking for a job.

HOW TO KEEP YOUR OPTIONS OPEN

If you decide on the stop-out route, make sure you keep your options open. Even if college isn't a priority now, it almost surely will be in the future.

1. If you know you will go to college after you take your year (or two) off, apply to college before you stop out—if you know which college you really want to go to. If it is possible, try to lock in your financial

aid package. However, Associate Dean of Admissions Linda Miller says that at UVA this isn't possible. "As far as scholarship money for the student who defers—we don't have merit scholarship funds. Our scholarships are all needs-based, and all financial aid has to be refiled every year." This is probably true for most colleges, but your chances are good that in a year or two you will still qualify for financial aid.

2. Some schools will not honor a deferment and will simply put you back in the pool of applicants the following year. You will have to decide if you are willing to risk the possibility of not getting into your first-choice college the next time around.

3. If the college says you will have to reapply after stopping out, find out what your chances will be of getting accepted. Keep records of all correspondence.

4. Keep your college informed about your plans. If you will be traveling, make sure there is some way for you to collect your mail. You don't want to miss deadlines just because nobody was around to pick up your mail.

5. If you decide not to apply to college right away, take the College Boards (SATs) or the ACTs before you graduate from high school. If you don't do as well as you think you can, you will have a chance to take them again and you will know what to expect. Make certain your school file is up-to-date and accessible from your high school guidance department.

6. Keep abreast of deadlines if you intend to apply to college during the year you have stopped out. If you don't you may find yourself out of school longer than you planned.

7. Keep lines of communication open with your parents and friends.

A Need To Prove Oneself

Doug Leonard from Northampton, Massachusetts, knew by the middle of his sophomore year in high school that he didn't want to go to college right away. At that stage of his life, school wasn't a high priority, and his grades often reflected his lack of interest.

"Actually," he admits, "I wanted to quit school altogether. I'd felt I'd had enough." His parents did not take kindly to this. They pointed out that quitting high school would have very serious consequences. "You'll be cutting yourself off from all kinds of jobs," they cautioned. "And if you do decide you ever want to go to college, you'll have a very hard time getting in without a high school diploma."

Of course, Doug knew his parents were right. But his desire to get away from school was so strong that he checked with his guidance counselor to find the quickest way to graduate. "I wanted time to think about who I really was, and what I wanted to do with myself."

Once Doug figured out how to graduate a year early, he really put his mind to it. He took the SATs and was surprised to find that despite some problems with dyslexia, he'd scored quite well. That was important. First, it sent a signal to his parents that he was stopping out and not "dropping out."

Second, Doug was keeping his options open. When he decided he was ready to apply to college, his test scores would be on file. Six months after he turned 16, Doug received his high school diploma and

"I wanted time to think about who I really was, and what I wanted to do with myself."

was eager to look for a job. "I wanted to prove that I could be something besides a student."

COMMON THREADS

If there is one thing these stories have in common, it is that regardless of what motivated these people to put their college education on hold, each displayed an independent spirit. Even if some of them were not successful in gaining parental approval for their decisions, all tried to keep communication lines open. Says Leana, "Now that I've taken the year off, my dad talks it up with his friends who have college-bound kids." In fact, most of these parents finally agreed with their children's choices, especially when they saw that they were acting in responsible ways.

Chapter III

No More Pencils, No More Books: Work After School Or, All That Glitters Is Hard To Get

IF YOU USE YOUR TIME AWAY FROM SCHOOL TO WORK, YOU CAN RUN INTO ALL KINDS OF PROBLEMS YOU NEVER DREAMED EXISTED. Leana remarks, "I'd never worked a forty-hour week before. It's a whole different world. School was fun. Work lasts from nine to five, and that's not always fun."

Sometimes the job that sounds great doesn't work out at all. The reasons may seem mysterious and frightening. As a first-time employee, you may not understand what's expected of you on the job, or you may find that you haven't thought through what you really want from your time out. Sometimes you and your employer simply won't get along, or perhaps there won't be enough work for you to do.

Problems may arise in the workplace, in your living situation, in how you use your free time, or in how you handle your money. Check back to see how you responded to some of the items in the self-assessment in Chapter I that have to do with short-term goals, ability to use leisure time, and ability to get along with people different from yourself. You may find that these are areas that are worth tracking even before difficulties arise. You probably won't be able to solve all your problems this way, but at least you may develop an understanding of why things can go wrong. As you read through the chapters that deal with working, you'll see how different people responded to difficult situations. Perhaps the coping strategies developed by others will work for you. Just being aware of potential trouble spots can be an advantage.

MAKE A PLAN

You're probably tired of everyone telling you to make a plan, but do it anyway. In fact, make lots of plans—before you finish high school, if possible. Then be ready to scrap or modify them as you gain new insights and experience. Plans don't have to be elaborate, but they do have to be more complex than, "I plan not to have anything to do with school for one entire year." While getting away from school routines may be a driving factor in your stopping out, that, in itself, is not the plan. The plan will be what you do during that year or two.

You don't necessarily need a five-page, single-spaced, typed set of objectives and goals. You can make a plan for what you'd like to learn from a job or how much you expect to earn (and save) over the year. You can make a plan for how you will spend your earnings—what specific goodies you would like to own now that you will have your own money. You can plan to save for a trip or to put money away for college. You can make a plan for how you intend to spend your leisure time. Or, if you plan to do any traveling, when and where do you expect to go? The more thought you give to your time out, the more likely it is that you will be satisfied with what you've done. You are the only one of you there is, and if you don't take yourself seriously, no one else will either.

JOB OPTIONS

If you decide that at least part of your time out will be spent working, you need to figure out how to get a job when you have no job experience. Most entry-level jobs aren't glamorous, and they don't pay very well. With a little luck, however, it won't take long to find your first job if you aren't picky. Even if the first job you get isn't what you want, you will learn something from it. Future employers will be impressed that you were able to work at even a dull job because it will show that you are a serious worker. There are also employers out there who are looking for people to train into responsible positions. So before you start job hunting, figure out what you want from your work experience.

1. Think about two or three areas in which you'd like to work and the reasons why.

2. Gather information. Check with family, friends, teachers, and guidance counselors to see if they can help you. If your best friend's mom says, "Oh, my brother-in-law owns a sporting goods store, would you like me to find out if he can use a stock person?" say "yes" if this is something you'd like. You'd be surprised how many people get jobs because they know someone who needs help.

3. Read the Help Wanted sections in the newspaper every day. Answer every ad that looks promising.

4. Register with the local State Employment Service. (It's in the White Pages of the telephone book in your state's government section.) Once you register with the employment service, you will be allowed to log onto their computers to find jobs that are listed with them.

5. Check out your local Youth Bureau, if your community has one. Often it has unusual jobs listed for young people.

6. Make a list of local businesses you are interested in working for. Do you know anyone who works there? If so, check to see if he or she will put in a good word for you. Are there businesses you frequent? Do you know the boss? You can stop in and talk to him or her directly.

7. Phoning a place of business cold can be pretty scary, but you can also get lucky. So call first and ask for the name of the person in charge of hiring. Try to set up an interview.

8. Find out what kind of clothes are appropriate for the job and wear them for the interview. It is definitely a good idea to remove earrings from nose, lips, tongue, cheeks, etc. during interviews and during work. Spiked purple hair and torn jeans are not very likely to impress a prospective employer. But you already know that, right?

9. Have a resume ready to send to a prospective employer or bring one with you. Make certain that it is neatly typed and that there are absolutely NO TYPOS. Do get it typed on a computer, and have it Xeroxed on good white or off-white paper (not in day-glo orange, please). In the world of work you need to impress employers with your ability to fit in, not stand out.

10. If you are told you will have to wait to find out if you are hired, keep looking for other jobs, but don't be afraid to check back. Persistence often pays off.

11. Tell everyone you know that you are job hunting.

12. It is better to be specific about the kind of job you are interested in. Telling a prospective employer that "I'll do anything," means you haven't thought through your own specific skills or the kind of jobs the employer has to offer.

13. Look at job hunting as your job until someone hires you. That means you need to set up at least one job search task for yourself every day. If you don't have an interview lined up, stop off at the employment service or a temp agency or head for your library and read some books on how to conduct a job search.

14. Job hunting is exhausting—and sometimes filled with disappointment. Take time out to do something nice for yourself, or volunteer at an organization for a couple hours a week. It will make you feel needed.

15. Don't get discouraged. You will land a job.

HOW TO WRITE A RESUME

A resume is not your autobiography. It is a one-page advertisement of your capabilities. It shows a prospective employer that you are the person he or she should hire. Of course, you may think you haven't accomplished enough to fill up even one page of a blank piece of paper. But if you stop and think about what you've done so far, you may surprise yourself.

A resume has three parts: education, work experience, and activities. You probably think you don't have work experience. You are, after all, looking for your first job. So let's start at the beginning. At the top and center of the page, put your name, address, telephone number, and e-mail address, if you have one. Drop down a couple of spaces. On the left-hand side, in capital letters, type "EDUCATION." Underneath that put your high school and the year you graduated. Underneath that put any honors you have earned, such as how often you made the honor roll. Include such things as offices held and club memberships that might have a bearing on the job you are looking for, such as member of food service club or member of 4-H fashion club, etc. One young man I talked to mentioned during an interview that he'd had perfect attendance in high school for all four years! Now that really impressed the interviewer. He figured that this was one worker who wouldn't call in sick just because he had a sore toe. Don't pad this section, but do think about your achievements. This isn't the time to be modest.

In the next section type "EXPERIENCE." At this point in your life, you probably have little work experience. However, you may have had a summer job as a camp counselor, or you may have worked in child care. You can list part-time work you have done for various neighbors—house painting, gardening. Again, don't pad this, but do include any paid work you have done. And if you have had experience in setting up a Web page for one of your parents or for a friend—or yourself, be sure to mention that.

The third section is where you can list your "ACTIVITIES." Have you done some community service work through your school, church, or synagogue? As a member of your school community, did you take part in any unusual activities, such as fundraising to take a trip with your Spanish or French class to Mexico City or Paris? Did your bike group pedal 200 miles to the New Jersey Pine Barrens? Did you work with your school lunch program to get better food? Did you work on a special law project in your school? In other words, think about things that make you stand apart from other job applicants—and to show that you will be a diligent worker.

Later on, as you build more job experience, get a college degree, and take part in internship programs, you will drop the stuff you did in high school from your resume. For now, however, these things are important. One other thing: you may say, "references upon request." Before you give out the name of a person you wish to speak on your behalf, you must call that person and ask if you may use his or her name. Also, you will want to be sure that if you give a person's name to a prospective employer, that reference will say good things about you. You don't want a reference to say, "You want to hire Joe? I wouldn't do that! He did a terrible job on my garden last summer."

Jane Levine

924 North Wood Avenue

Linden, New Jersey 07666

Phone: 201/555-4184

E-mail: applicant@aol.com

■ EDUCATION:

Linden High School
Graduated: June, 1999
Honor roll: 4th and 5th marking period, 1997-98
    1st, 3rd, 4th marking period, 1998
Senior Class Treasurer: 1998-99—Responsible for handling all finances
    for senior class trip to Montreal, as well as for keeping the books
    for the senior prom.
Associate Editor, class yearbook: 1998-99—Wrote the descriptions of
    various clubs and school organizations.
Spanish Club award for best translation into Spanish of *My Father's
Dragon* (a children's book).

■ EXPERIENCE:

Junior counselor, "Y" Day Camp, Elizabeth, New Jersey, Summers
    1997, 1998. Ran the arts and craft shop in 1998. I was responsible
    for helping children work in leather and clay and with wood-working
    equipment. Also fired all ceramic pieces.
Child care for several families in neighborhood: 1995-present.

■ ACTIVITIES:

Volunteered two evenings a week at the soup kitchen during my senior
    year of high school.
Volunteered at my Temple to tutor Bar and Bat Mitzvah students in
    Hebrew: 1996 and 1997.

■ SKILLS:

Typing: familiar with Microsoft Word, can work on either Macintosh or
    IBM computers.
Reading and speaking knowledge of Spanish. Reading knowledge of
    Hebrew.

■ REFERENCES:

Available upon request.

Keep a copy of your resume on hand so that you can change and update it as you gain more experience. Every time you make a change, be sure to check your spelling.

MORE REASONS TO TAKE TIME OUT

There are many reasons to take a break between high school and college. Many have to do with the desire to become independent.

A Plan To Establish Independence

When Rachel Reinitz, of Geneva, New York, was 14, her dad died. With a younger brother and sister in the wings, she decided to finish high school in three years and go right to college. She was admitted to Carnegie Mellon University with an excellent financial aid package. But the more she thought about rushing off to college, the less attractive it sounded. She decided to take a year off and work.

"I wanted to establish my independence and see if I could support myself if I needed to." The added challenge of living and working in New York City excited her. "I figured that if I could make it in New York City at 17, I wouldn't have to worry about making it anywhere."

Rachel made certain that her financial aid package would be safe for a year, then she discussed her plans with her mother, who expressed surprise but supported her daughter's decision to work.

Rachel decided to become an au pair—a live-in child care person in a private home. Instead of going through the classified ads in the newspapers, Rachel worked with an employment agency that specialized in child care situations. Although employment agencies require a fee for finding you a job, her employer paid it for her. Before making final arrangements, Rachel invited her mother to New York City to meet her at her employer's home. It turned out to be in a beautiful old brownstone right on Park Avenue.

"I had my own separate room with a shared bath. My quarters were once the maid's quarters—small, but private." There was even a pull-out bed for a guest. Rachel's duties were carefully spelled out in writing and signed by both Rachel and her employer so that there would be no misunderstandings. She had weekends off, several evenings off, as well as free time when the two children were in school. There were some other chores, as well.

"I accomplished the main thing I set out to do, emotionally and mentally. I was completely independent—except for medical and dental bills. I loved living in New York. Even though my salary was not huge, I had enough money from my job to go to theaters and museums. My friends, who were in nearby colleges, would come to visit. I even had time to take a couple of courses at Hunter College—and it was there I decided I'd major in engineering."

A Plan That Evolves

Philip Bereaud of Danby, New York, decided not to make a plan when he finished high school. "I thought I'd be too much like everyone else," he says. So at first he lived in his father's house until he found a job as a dishwasher in a local restaurant. As soon as he could, he moved into an apartment with a couple of older guys. "And then," he says, "I realized that my life was just as much a routine as when I was in school. It was just a different routine."

When a friend mentioned he was driving out to Oregon, Philip jumped at the opportunity to join him. While this seemed like a pretty irresponsible thing to do, Philip's real plan over the next two years grew out of his willingness to take chances and leave himself open to all kinds of new ideas.

Once Philip was in Oregon, he attended the trial of some social activists. Among those on trial was his traveling companion, Tim. There were thirteen people—all part of a group called the Cathedral Force Action Group—on trial. They'd been arrested because they tried to prevent a logging company from cutting down the old growth trees (known as "Cathedral trees") in a national forest.

"There was such a range of people on trial," Philip says. "Some were like Tim, who is a real hippie, and there were people who were clean shaven and in suits. There were those who looked really wise—a whole variety of people."

The trial made Philip think that if people were willing to risk jail for the sake of trees, there must be something to what they were doing. Fortunately, none of the thirteen was given a jail sentence. All were given probation.

■ The Plan Evolves

Philip wanted to find out more. He decided to learn firsthand about the problems we are facing in our environment. Without realizing it, Philip was developing a plan for himself.

He joined a group called EarthFirst!. With about two hundred others, Philip helped set up a camp in the woods in an effort to save a wilderness area called Oak Flats. Their goal was to draw attention to the problem of the diminishing national forests.

Philip says, "This is our land, and unless the public knows what's happening to it, the balance between timber, wildlife, and recreation and research will be destroyed." The camp attracted a lot of media attention—something that environmentalists know is important to their cause.

When the camp closed, Philip signed up to harvest fir cones. Just as he was finishing this job, he learned that there were dangerous forest fires to the south. He joined the firefighters who were putting out the fires among smoldering stumps. "We had to dig up the stumps and grind out the fires for twelve hours a day," he says.

Through these diverse experiences, Philip learned to get along with and understand the viewpoint of two completely different groups of people. When he was with the environmental group, he was associating with those who wished to be "at one" with the earth, and take as little as possible from it. When he was with the cone pickers and firefighters, Philip worked with those who saw the woods as a place to make money.

"At first I couldn't understand how a person could look at a tree and see money. But I learned when I was cone picking to look at a tree and say, 'Well, five bushels of cones are in that tree. It's a $50 tree.' And that's the way loggers do it. They look at a tree and say, 'Oh, that tree is so many board feet.'"

Not All Plans Work Out

Remember Sue Schwartz from Chapter II? She wanted very much to volunteer in Zimbabwe but kept getting turned down. Although she tried to keep her spirits up during the first five months by working, it was a pretty discouraging time for Sue.

When the chance to go to Nepal arrived, she grabbed it. Sue's experience in Nepal turned out to be less than she had hoped it would be. Part of it, she says, was her own lack of preparation. "I didn't do much research before I went to Nepal. I was very idealistic. I was just 17 at the time and really believed that I could change the world." On balance, however, Sue felt her five months in Nepal had its good points. "I taught English as a second language, I worked on a kindergarten project that Educate the Children was doing, and I worked in the villages, too." But Educate the Children is a very small operation. Sue realized that students volunteering through larger organizations had opportunities that were not available to her. The larger organizations arranged for their volunteers to meet interesting people who were working on diverse projects. "Everything that happened to me I did for myself."

Sue also learned some lessons about development work in Third World countries. "I was disillusioned for quite a while because so much foreign money is wasted. I was upset because people in the United States don't think in broader terms about their own way of living. I went to Nepal to learn how to help people—to learn what's right and what's wrong, what's condescending and what's not."

Over the five months she spent in Nepal, Sue wrote her parents many letters. She also kept a journal. When she came back to the United States, she was able to use one of the letters she wrote home as part of a college admission essay.

DEALING WITH REAL LIFE PROBLEMS

Making New Friends

Many who stop out to work find that making new friends and keeping old ones can be a major problem. This is especially true if the job you take is in food service or other low-paying fields.

Leana commented that all of her good friends were away at college. During her year out she worried that she was missing out on something. Rachel says, "The main difficulty I had was that I was lonely." Even though she took two classes at Hunter College, and her work with the children was time consuming, she had to fight loneliness and boredom.

Doug thought that one of the worst things about the two years he stopped out was that "I didn't meet anyone. I made no friends of lasting quality. It was a lonely time. I'm a person who needed to work in a public place and be around people. I missed making friends. My old high school friends were making new friends (at college), while I was in a rut."

Not everyone experiences a lack of friends. Matt had a lot of friends who had either dropped out of high school or didn't want to go to college. "People just sort of hung out together," he says. For years, work was the most important thing in Matt's life. "I was so eager to get into the rat race." Gradually, however, as Matt progressed about

Keeping Old Friends, Making New Ones

No matter how happy you are not to go off to college, it can be pretty depressing to watch your friends leave for someplace that promises to be exciting. Here are some tips from those who have "been there."

- *Don't lose contact with your old friends. Even if they go away to college, keep up a correspondence via e-mail, letters, or by phone.*

- *Plan visits with special friends at college.*

- *If you are staying in your hometown, join at least one organization in your community that has regular meetings.*

- *Take part in church or other group activities that are fun.*

- *Become a "big brother" or "big sister" to an elementary school kid.*

- *During the times you are really lonely, do something special for yourself.*

- *Remember when you are on the job, you are being paid to work, no matter how small your salary. Keep your socializing to a minimum. If you do make friends on the job, consider it a bonus.*

- *In the beginning, be a keen observer of how your coworkers relate to one another.*

as far as he could go in the restaurant business, the pals he'd hung out with became less interesting to him.

GETTING FIRED—WHEN TO QUIT

In the real world, lots of people get fired or laid off from their jobs. Anyone who shows up for work on Friday only to be told it will be his or her last day, goes home angry and depressed. Even when the boss assures you it isn't your fault, or even when you didn't like the job in the first place, getting fired is a definite downer. You will want to leave the workplace quickly (after picking up your last paycheck). The last thing in the world you need is for your coworkers to see you in a shaken state.

You may not feel like telling your parents or your friends that you lost your job. But actually, you will feel better almost immediately when you do. For one thing, virtually anyone who has ever worked has gotten fired. By discussing your situation with people close to you, you will soon realize that getting fired is not a tragedy. It is simply a glitch in your plans. It doesn't mean you are a failure. It does mean, however, that you will have to look for a new job. It is sort of like falling off a horse or your bicycle. The sooner you get back on, the stronger you'll be. But before you start job hunting, you may want to rethink your work goals so you don't wind up in a similar situation.

Back on the Street

Shortly after he started working as a dishwasher at a local restaurant, Doug was fired. "That was a hard thing," he says. At 16 finding a job hadn't been easy, and working made him feel great. "I wasn't fired for being inefficient or indifferent. I was fired because the manager had overhired." Still, it hurt. Nevertheless, he learned that even a little experience was enough to land him a job in a better restaurant. A few months later, however, he realized that this wasn't where he wanted to be. But Doug also learned that he couldn't just walk away from a job because he'd had a bad day.

If You Lose Your Job

- *According to Richard Nelson Bolles, author of* What Color Is Your Parachute?, *losing a job is part of the real world. He says that the average worker has to job hunt at least eight times during his or her lifetime. And that estimate is for people who are building careers, not for teenagers looking for work!*

- *Sometimes there is no rhyme or reason for why you get fired.*

- *If you have worked at a job for at least three months (even part-time), check with your state unemployment agency to see if you are eligible for unemployment insurance benefits while you are in between jobs.*

- *Try to maintain an optimistic attitude while you are job hunting.*

- *Try to find at least one person who will give you a good reference from your last job.*

- *Think about the kinds of jobs that may offer you a challenge.*

- *Make looking for a new job a top priority, and job hunt every single weekday. But remember, no one can job hunt for eight hours a day.*

- *If you are worried about money, work for a temporary agency for a couple of days a week until you land the job you want. Often a temp job can turn into a full-time one. Temporary agencies can be found in the Yellow Pages of the phone book under "Employment Agencies," in the Help Wanted pages of your newspaper, and on the Internet.*

"There was one moment that I recall as a striking means of grow-ing up. It was a hard day, and I was exhausted. I was angry at the boss and the people I was working with. I wanted to quit. Suddenly, I real-ized that if I quit, I wouldn't eat. I probably could have gotten money from my parents; I knew I didn't want to do that. I couldn't quit for my own peace of mind.

"That was a specific moment in my life. And it was a very power-ful experience."

Not long after this bad day, Doug landed a more satisfying job as a mechanic in the bicycle shop where he had bought all of his bike equipment since he was a little kid. He was able to convince the owner to hire him because he showed him that he had kept a job—even one he didn't especially like. He worked at the bicycle shop until he went off to college and then got hired back during summer breaks.

Matt got fired from a restaurant job he'd planned on quitting any-way. "The boss and I had a personality conflict, and I had already lined up another job but not for another two weeks. But I was relieved when she fired me—although, of course, I'd rather have had the extra two weeks' pay and the chance to quit first."

Leana also got fired from her first job as a bagger in a supermar-ket. "Even when it's a job you don't like, you are hurt when the boss fires you," she says. But that experience made Leana realize that it was important to look for work that offered her a challenge. She reviewed her reasons for stopping out and used her knowledge of Japanese to land a job in a Buddhist publishing firm in a nearby town. "I did every-thing—running accounts, bookkeeping, and shipping. I loved being around books and got along well with the woman I was working for. Even though I only got minimum wage, it was an excellent experience."

Chapter IV

Am I Having Fun Yet? Nuts & Bolts Of Making The Most Of Your Time Out

WHOSE MONEY IS IT ANYWAY?

OK, YOU'VE GOT THAT JOB. It looks as if things are really going according to plan. Gosh, though, the paycheck is smaller than you thought it was going to be.

How come? Well, along with your proof of citizenship, you had to fill out one of those Federal Government W-4 forms, right?

Lesson 1: the money you earn over your lifetime isn't really all yours. The Feds take out taxes, unemployment insurance, and social security. In most states there is an additional amount removed for state taxes. What's left is all yours. Well, not quite. You may find yourself with some fixed expenses.

If you live at home, you might be contributing something to household expenses on a monthly basis. As a newly minted bonafide grown-up wage-earner, it is appropriate to contribute to family expenses if you wish to have a say in things that affect your home life. The more open you and your family are in the beginning about what is expected of you, the fewer misunderstandings will occur later on.

If you aren't asked to make a financial contribution to the family budget, you can figure out other ways to contribute to family life.

Leana's mother felt that she should save as much as possible for college. But Leana did contribute her time. "I pitched in with household chores," she says. "And I spent a lot of time with my younger half-brother and half-sister."

Aaron Seymour decided saving money by living at home was more important than living independently while he was with the Conservation Corps in Pittsfield, Massachusetts. "AmeriCorps pays just $5.86 an hour for a 30-hour week," he says, even though he became a supervisor of a crew of eleven people his second year. He did contribute to the family food budget but was still able to bank a portion of his pay regularly.

Doug also lived at home, rent-free, for three months until he'd saved some money. He loves to cook and did a major share of the cooking for his family. Then he and a friend decided to share an apartment. "But," he says, "rent was more than we could afford, even with two salaries. We found a suitable place with three bedrooms and advertised for a third housemate." In the beginning Doug found that most of his paycheck went towards apartment expenses.

Nate Kipp was able to save several thousand dollars over the two years he worked with Habitat for Humanity through AmeriCorps. He was very focused on what he wanted from his working experience. "I was able to save a lot of money," says Nate, "because I know how to live cheaply. The first year I was with Habitat in Florida, I lived in a work camp. This year I'm at a Habitat site in Cleveland, and I'm living in a Catholic Worker Community, which is low cost. I am not a Catholic, but this is a very good situation. A few others of us live in this community. We pay minimal rent, and we get our food. People take turns cooking. We live with a total of 15 people. This can be difficult at times, but we manage to talk our differences out."

Sooner or later you will move out on your own. Before you do, think carefully about your goals for stopping out. Being financially independent is a laudable goal, but renting an apartment and choosing housemates can be a minefield, especially the first few times. Here are some suggestions from those with battle scars.

HOW TO RENT AN APARTMENT AND CHOOSE HOUSEMATES

1. Read your lease carefully before signing it. Better yet, take it home and have a parent or other adult read it over with you.

2. Know what you are getting: Can you add housemates? Will you have to pay for utilities? (If you live in a cold climate, winter heating bills can eat up your entire paycheck. The same is true if you are in a very hot climate and run the air conditioner day and night.) Are pets allowed? If you don't agree with certain clauses, discuss them with your landlord before you sign to see if he or she will delete them. Make sure the deletions are on both copies of the lease.

3. Don't sign a lease unless all housemates do so, and make sure you are responsible for only your share of the rent—even if one of them moves out.

4. Understand the terms of your security deposit—usually a portion of a month's rent which is to be refunded if you haven't done any damage to the place. If you notice holes in the walls, cracked or broken tops, marks on the floor, write it all down on a piece of paper and date it before you move in. Give one copy to your landlord and keep one along with your lease. When your lease is up, if there is no additional damage, you should get your security deposit back—with interest. If you or your housemates have put holes in the walls, ripped up the car-

peting, etc., you will be charged for repairs. All too often those repairs take up your entire deposit, so treat your apartment with respect.

5. Try to sign as short a lease as possible. Better yet, none at all. Be sure that if you have to leave before your lease is up, you can sublet your part of the apartment.

6. Best friends don't always make the best housemates. This comment was made by several people.

7. When you get the phone installed, get all housemates' names on the phone bill. Make sure you have everyone's home address, so that if one person skips out without paying a bill, you've got a place to contact him or her—or the person's parents.

8. Make it a rule not to lend money to any housemates, no matter how well you know them. You may wind up losing both a friend and your money. The same thing applies to you: don't borrow money from your housemates.

9. Take the time to meet with all your housemates and discuss all ground rules. Especially important is determining when bills are to be paid. Even if your housemates are late with rent, phone, or utility bills, be sure to send in your share on time.

10. Set up strict guidelines regarding overnight visitors. If you don't do this in the beginning, you will find that you've acquired a nonpaying permanent guest who eats all your food, uses your shampoo, burns out your hair dryer, is always in your way, and is probably a slob.

11. Make sure that you and your housemates are in agreement on who is responsible for cleaning up common areas—kitchen, living room, and bathroom.

12. Be sure everyone understands rules of privacy and keeps out of your room and other personal space.

13. Keep valuables locked up.

14. Take out renter's insurance. It is generally inexpensive and could save you a great deal of money if your apartment is broken into

or there is a fire. NOTE: Few young people take this particular piece of advice until after something important, such as a bicycle, is stolen.

A WORD ABOUT USING CREDIT CARDS

Almost anyone can get a credit card these days—even if you don't earn much money. If you are a student when you apply for a credit card, you will have offers from virtually every credit card company in America. Credit card companies love to have you owe them money. In fact, the more you owe, the more credit card companies will want your business. And why not? After all, they make upwards of 18 to 20 percent a year on your unpaid balance. Of course having a credit card definitely makes a person feel very grown up. Who doesn't like to go out to a restaurant with a girl or boy friend, order a fine meal, pick up the check, and pay it with a credit card? After all, hasn't the credit card company given you thousands of dollars of credit?

Mmmmm—just remember that as the owner of that card YOU are responsible for paying off all the charges you run up, plus interest. So while it's tempting to run around charging all kinds of goodies on that card, there is always a day of reckoning. Sure, when you receive the monthly bill, you are given a minimum amount that you have to pay—one 36th of the total bill. If you don't make a substantial payment each month, and keep running up bills, you will soon find yourself deep in credit card debt. Joe King, credit counselor at the Cornell Finger Lakes Credit Union in Ithaca, New York, estimates that one in four Americans wind up in serious credit card debt. Don't let it happen to you. The pattern of spending that you develop while you are young could trip you up later on in life. So while credit cards are a fact of life, and are useful, you need to be very cautious when using them.

Joe King is the person many people who get over their heads in credit card debt come to for help. This is what he says:

1. Be discriminating when you are deciding which credit card offers to accept.

2. The first thing to look for is the federal disclosure information on the back of the offer. Yes, it is usually in small print, but read that small print carefully. (This information is required by law.) Try to avoid credit cards that have an annual fee. Don't accept a card that has a two cycle balancing method for computing your average daily interest. In a two tier system you are charged not only the interest on last month's unpaid balance, but also on your new purchases as well. In effect, you are being charged for two months at once. So while the interest rate may appear to be only 4.9 percent or so, you are really paying much more. The most common payment plan is simply the average daily balance—which is computed on a 30-day cycle. Also, the disclosure box carries the "teaser" offer at a very low interest rate. Be sure to see what the rate will change to after six months. Look for grace periods, normally 25 days.

3. Keep your credit limit low as long as you are a low wage earner or a student.

4. Establish a savings account before you apply for a credit card. You can use that account as collateral when applying for a card.

5. As a new credit card applicant, you may have to get a parent or other relative to co-sign for your card. But if you get behind on your payments, it reflects on the co-signee as well. You don't want to be responsible for another person getting a bad credit rating because of your problem.

6. The secret to establishing a good credit rating is to pay on your account monthly, and pay it on time.

7. You can take a cash advance by using your credit card, but remember that the interest on a cash advance starts immediately, unlike the grace period when you purchase goods. And there may be a separate fee for a cash advance.

8. Before you make a purchase with your credit card ask yourself if you NEED it or if you WANT it. Also, is this item a good value in terms of how often you will use it? If you don't NEED the item, but WANT it, try SAVING for it.

9. When you receive your monthly bill, check each and every item. If you see an error, call the 800 number on the back of your card and tell them about the error. Be sure to follow up with any more information you have.

10. Don't let anyone borrow your card—ever.

11. Don't give your credit card number out over the phone unless it is to a very reputable catalogue company.

12. Be sure to make a monthly budget. The five most important areas of expenses to pay first are: housing, utilities, food, transportation, AND yourself. Make saving a priority.

13. If you find yourself with too much credit card debt, call the credit card company and tell them you cannot meet the payments. Try to negotiate a lower monthly fee—and cut up your card until you get caught up.

14. If you still can't get straightened out, find a reputable credit counselor and get help.

PUTTING MONEY ASIDE

Unless you've grossly miscalculated, you will have some money left from each paycheck. Regardless of what your plans are for that money, you will probably want to open a savings account and perhaps a checking account.

If you are under 18, you may be surprised to learn that while all banks will be happy to let you put money into a savings account, not all of them will let you open a checking account. Said one bank manager, "Checking accounts can be a liability. Most young people don't know the basics of balancing a checkbook." Still, if you have a job, act like a serious person, and can demonstrate your need for a checking account, you can usually find a bank that will accommodate you.

TIPS ON BANKING

1. Most banks require that you keep a minimum balance in checking and savings accounts, so wait until you have several hundred dollars before you make that initial deposit. In fact, some banks actually deduct money from your savings account if you go below their minimum balance! It's a good idea to shop around for the best deal. Many people report that credit unions are the most user-friendly, although not always in the best location or with the best hours.

2. If you have a steady job, you may be able to arrange for a direct-deposit checking account, with your employer sending your paycheck directly to your bank.

3. Your automatic teller card frequently doubles as a bank credit card. This is convenient when shopping because you won't have to show identification. But it is not a real charge card. The money is taken directly out of your account, so when you use the card, be sure to enter the transaction in your checkbook. Do not ever let this card out of your possession, and don't let anyone else use it.

4. If you lose your card, report it to a bank official immediately.

5. If you withdraw more than is in your account, the automatic teller machine will eat your card.

6. Learn how to balance your checkbook and reconcile it with your bank statement each and every month. Remember, both you and the bank can make mistakes. If you have a problem, see a bank official immediately.

7. Make it a policy to put even a small amount of your paycheck in a savings account every pay day. "Even when I was working just part-time," says Dan Wallner, "I decided I'd never miss $25 a month, so that's how I started my savings account."

"I decided I'd never miss $25 a month, so that's how I started my savings account."

KEEPING TRACK OF YOUR MONEY

If you don't make some sort of a budget, your money will be gone in a minute. The easy part is making the budget. The difficult part is sticking to it. So before you rush to move away from home, decide how you will spend your paycheck.

■ **Housing:**

How much you pay for housing will vary from place to place. But even in large, expensive cities, you can find reasonable rents, if you are willing to share your living space. Again, it depends upon your goals. Nate didn't think living in an apartment was important, so he was willing to explore alternative living arrangements while working in AmeriCorps.

Ryan Everhart, another AmeriCorps worker who served on a low-income housing project in Raleigh, North Carolina, found living on such a limited budget—$660 a month—too restricting. In addition to the 50 hours a week he put in with AmeriCorps, he also waited tables for ten hours a week at a local college eatery. This also gave him a chance to meet people his own age.

One way to cut housing costs is to share an apartment or a house with several people. Check your local paper under listings such as "Housemate Wanted."

■ Food:

This expense varies according to place, season, appetite, and how many times you get invited out to a free dinner. One hundred fifty dollars a month is probably a modest amount and doesn't take into account snacks, lunches at work, an occasional dinner out, or that inevitable late-night pizza. Paying for all of your own meals is a lot different from when you lived and ate at home.

> "Paying for all of your own meals is a lot different from when you lived and ate at home."

Tip: Buy a good basic cookbook and learn to make things from scratch. Make enough for leftovers. Doug says, "I used to buy a whole chicken and roast it. I'd put half in the freezer. That way I'd have a couple of meals during the week." Also, get your mom's best recipes for basic stuff like spaghetti with meatballs and macaroni and cheese. Keep staples like big jars of peanut butter and jelly on hand.

Tip: Bring lunch and snacks to work from home. Expensive lunches out can totally ruin your budget—and your waistline. "One of the good things about working in food service is that you get at least one meal free," says Matt.

■ **Transportation:**

Is your job within walking distance of your home? Can you use a bike to get around town? Is public transportation readily available? Travel to and from work can be expensive, so be sure to figure it into your budget.

■ **Recreation:**

Will you be able to afford a movie once or twice a month? Do you have to pay for cable TV? Do you or one of your housemates have a VCR so you can rent videos and share the cost? Are there plays and concerts you want to go to? Once you know how much (or how little) you can budget each month for recreation, you may be very happy to just

Other things you might consider:

- *Membership at a local "Y" or health club. You might put this on your wish list of birthday or Christmas or Hanukkah presents.*
- *Discount tickets to plays.*
- *Find out if you can usher at special sporting events or concerts in exchange for a free ticket.*
- *Keep a wish list handy to give out to family and friends who may be generous at gift-giving times.*

get together with a couple of friends, or invite them over to your place. (Have them bring the snacks.)

Weekends: Use weekends to get together with friends to bike or hike or backpack. Share transportation costs when traveling by car.

■ **Personal Items:**

When you lived at home, many personal items were provided for you. Now you are responsible for little things that add up to a lot more money than you ever thought: toothbrushes, laundry soap, toilet paper, etc. And bigger items such as that bargain sweater you spotted in the department store. And you, too, will have to keep track of birthdays and other gift-giving occasions of friends and relatives. You are responsible for phone bills, too. You can probably count on most of the clothes already hanging in your closet, but eventually you will need to replace a number of basic items. All of these things need to be factored into your budget. Many of those who spend their year or two out in the working world learn to frequent the thrift shops for great bargains. Says Rachel, "Learning to live on a budget is an important part of growing up and becoming independent."

■ **Health Insurance:**

This is a major problem for young people. Most entry-level jobs and jobs in small businesses won't have any sort of health insurance for young workers. Your best bet is to see if you can stay on your parents' health plans until you become a student again. Most health insurance plans have some sort of a COBRA (Consolidated Omnibus Budget Reconciliation Act) plan that allows a parent to maintain a child who reaches the age of 18 (and is not in college) on their medical plan for a year or so for a separate monthly fee.

> "Learning to live on a budget is an important part of growing up."

Checklist for Making a Monthly Budget

Unless you are a person who really loves little boxes and lots of numbers, making a monthly budget can be a bore. It is a good idea to keep your consumer desires to a minimum. Don't get sucked into buying things on credit. You've got plenty of time to develop those expensive tastes—save them for when you have money to indulge yourself. Here are the major things to keep on top of, and review every two or three months:

- *Your monthly income after taxes and the dates you get paid*
- *Date the rent is due*
- *Date the gas and electric bills are due*
- *Last day to pay the phone bill*
- *Monthly cable bill*
- *Weekly food costs*
- *Adding to your wardrobe*
- *Adding to your CD or book collection*
- *Necessary items to keep your living space in order*
- *Special events that require money*
- *Unexpected expenses*
- *Savings*

Keep your checklist in a prominent place—taped to the wall above your desk, on the refrigerator, or next to your calendar. Keep close track of your expenses so you know where your money is going.

Final Thoughts: You need to be aware of items that are one-time costs and those which are ongoing. If the phone company or electric company require a deposit before they will connect you, keep all receipts. Sometimes if your parents have lived in your community for many years, the utility companies will waive the fees.

And don't forget that savings account. If you find your monthly expenses exceed your income, you may need to rethink plans for living away from home, look for a better-paying job, or, take a second job.

Becoming an independent person is exciting. You won't have anyone looking over your shoulder telling you how to manage your time when you are not working. But when you are at work, you have to remember your time belongs to the person who is paying you. How you conduct yourself at work or at play is totally up to you. That includes all the mistakes you make as well.

TIME ON YOUR HANDS AND NOT MUCH MONEY

What do people do when they're not sleeping, working, or eating? When you were a student, finding things to do with your leisure time wasn't difficult. If you weren't studying, you were hanging out with friends, partying, getting involved in sports or other school activities. In fact, there were probably so many things to do, you never had to think about free time: there wasn't any.

Now that you are a working person, there is no one to tell you what to do. You don't have any homework. You can come home from your job, check out the refrigerator, turn on the TV, and watch it for as long as you want. If you do this every day, you will, as Doug notes, "become totally lethargic. You'll lose sight of why you really wanted to take time out."

One problem is that you no longer have a ready-made community of like-minded people to do things with. You don't have a lot of bucks to spend on entertainment, and most of all, you will not feel as if you're ready to join into all of those sober, adult activities your parents do. So what kinds of things are out there for you? What is it that the young working person does with his or her time?

Doug says, "At first I watched lots of TV. After a while I began to feel awful. My mind felt like it was turning to mush. So I made sure to buy a newspaper every single day. Not only did it keep me in touch with what was going on in the world, but the local paper kept me abreast of day-to-day events in my hometown. And I discovered there were many things going on that were free."

As it turned out, just reading the newspaper wasn't enough intellectual stimulation for Doug. (Most newspapers are written for the reading level of a sixth grader.) "I began to realize that I really didn't know very much about world events, so I'd follow some aspect of current events in the paper for a while, and then I'd call up my high school social studies teacher and ask her to recommend some books for me to read." Eventually, Doug got so interested in American politics, that he audited a course at his local college.

Auditing College Classes and Other Ways to Learn

Many colleges and universities will allow you to audit courses for very little money if the professor agrees to let you sit in. Of course, you won't get the full benefit of your professor's teaching, since there are restrictions on what an auditor can and cannot do. Usually, but not always, papers you write won't receive the teacher's written criticism. You may take the tests but not receive a grade, and since you haven't paid the full tuition, you won't receive credit. Since there is not pressure to work for a grade, you are free to set your own limits on how much you wish to learn. You will really be in charge of your own education. Or, you can register as an "extra mural" student, pay full tuition for a course and work for college credit that you may be able to transfer to the college of your choice at a later date.

Reading or attending classes may not be all you can do with free time. Go back and check out that plan you made for use of leisure time.

Leana decided to expand her interest in Japanese culture. But since she worked with books all day long, she joined a martial arts class in karate. "The day I actually broke a board with my bare hand was so exciting," she says. "I learned so much about how to control my own body. I never knew what it was like to feel so strong."

"The day I actually broke a board with my bare hand was so exciting. I never knew what it was like to feel so strong."

And Rachel, who in addition to taking a class or two at Hunter College, decided she always wanted to know how to scuba dive. "I have no idea when I'll ever get to use this skill, but it's important for me to overcome obstacles. I felt that exploring the world that is underwater in a wet suit with a tank strapped to my back had to be a major accomplishment." Even though the course was expensive, Rachel felt it was a worthwhile expenditure.

There is an awful lot of great stuff out there after working hours, if you are willing to make the effort. The most difficult part of sampling new activities is that often you won't have friends to go with you. "That's the advantage of signing up for a class," says Margie Ainslee, a young woman from Washington, DC, who stopped out. "You don't have to go with anyone because you're doing it for yourself."

Taking Courses on the Internet

Jonathan Finlay couldn't find classes he was interested in at the local colleges at a time that was convenient for him. So he searched the Internet and found literally thousands of college and continuing education courses he could sign up for. "I'm interested in learning about computer programming and designing Web sites," he says. And he has had no trouble finding dozens of courses that would fit the bill. "Some courses cost as little as $5 a month, while others will run $1,200 or more a semester. Of course the very inexpensive courses don't give you very much in the way of help. They simply publish new exercises and give you very little feedback." What Jon likes is that the more serious courses offer the opportunity for the student to interact with the professor both by e-mail and by phone. "And the chat rooms give you an opportunity to actively communicate with other people who are taking the course." That, coupled with the fact that you can log on to the course anytime, makes taking courses on line a very attractive alternative to a person who may not be able to get to a college campus. "I can do this on my own time," he says, "although most on line courses give you a time limit in which you must finish the course. On line courses attract people who really want to learn—otherwise you won't keep up with the work." And, as with courses offered at colleges and universities, there is a grace period, where if you decide the course isn't what you really wanted, most, if not all of your tuition will be refunded.

LEISURE TIME SUGGESTIONS
FROM OTHERS WHO STOPPED OUT

1. "Keep your mind active. Make yourself read and debate the issues. If you aren't going to do that, you'll have trouble when you get into college."—Susan P. Staggers, former director of admissions, Mount Holyoke College

2. "A lot of what you do with your time depends upon where you are located. If you are in an urban setting, there are many cultural events available. On the other hand, you can also learn a lot if you're working in the Forest Service out in Idaho. The main thing I'd say is just don't stop reading. Reading is the whole process of communication. Keep in touch with the world."—Richard Pierson, dean of admissions, Clark University

3. "I took a course in teaching reading to illiterate adults, and then volunteered two evenings a week. It was the most rewarding thing I'd ever done."—Dick Lewis, Minneapolis, MN

4. "I had a hard time getting a job in a new town, so after I finished job hunting each day, I went down to the local political campaign headquarters, licked envelopes, and did other chores for my congressman's re-election campaign. I even organized a team of kids to get out some important mailings. I was appreciated for the work I did, and it felt good to be doing a necessary task. One of the things I really treasure is a personal thank-you letter from my congressman after he was re-elected."—Gloria Simon, Worcester, MA

5. "Every weekend in good weather, I'd get together with other bicyclists, and we'd ride around the countryside. Sometimes we'd do 75 to 100 miles in one day. It was a great way to meet people and keep in shape."—Karen Levine, Sandy Hook, NJ

6. "I trained to become a 'techie' at my local radio station—and decided I loved radio enough to major in communications when I finally went off to college."—Doug Leonard, Northhampton, MA

7. "I got really involved in the Big Sister program in my community. And now that I'm in college, I still write to my little sister. I'm somebody she looks up to." —Lisa Martin, Baltimore, MD

Was It Worth It?

"My work experience made me ready to try different kinds of things. I never thought I'd enjoy working in an office. But I liked dealing with customers." —Leana Horowitz

"I became so much more independent. I was not as intimidated by new situations. When I got to college, I had less trouble adjusting than did many of my classmates. And I had a lot more of an appreciation for school." —Rachel Reinitz

"In the long run, stopping out didn't make things better, but I learned not to worry so much." —Margie Ainslee

"At the time I stopped out, I found that work was more fulfilling than school. I couldn't figure out what I would study, so I thought school would be a waste. Working and living on my own was the best thing I could have done."— Chuck Bury

"College is a safe place. The real world is all about getting your next meal. My experience during the two years I stopped out taught me that I can get even a menial job and be satisfied. My friends who were students think school is hard. They see that when you're working, you have money. Well, I can tell you, it was hard to get."—Doug Leonard

"I loved working for a veterinarian, but I wasn't going to become a vet just by working for one. I needed to learn again. The jobs I had were all dead-end—so I decided to come back home and finish my bachelor's degree."—Nora Schmidt

WHERE ARE THEY NOW?

Many of the people interviewed for this book have kept in touch with me. Several went to school after stopping out for a year. Others took a much longer time to get themselves into college.

Rachel Reinitz completed a master's degree in engineering and now works for IBM in robotics.

Philip Bereaud spent more than five years traveling all over the United States, studying with Native Americans, working in Hawaii, playing guitar and other musical instruments in a variety of bands. Today he is studying music and composition at the Berklee College of Music in Boston.

Sue Schwartz returned from her five months in Nepal and had a difficult time readjusting to life back in the United States. She is now a sophomore at Ithaca College and has finally realized her dream to go to Zimbabwe. She has been working all summer in one of the local eateries and saving her money. She will do a year with the School for International Studies, where she will learn about international development. "One thing I learned in Nepal is that you can't go into a community and say, 'OK this is what you need—you could use a water tap, and five years later, people come back and see that the water tap isn't working. They say, 'why didn't you take care of that tap?' And the community leaders say, 'well, you're the one who built it, why don't you do it?' People have to want development. It has to come from the people."

Doug Leonard majored in communications at the University of North Carolina, Greensboro. He did some radio and television work and signed on to Teach for America, a branch of AmeriCorps, for two years. He now is a certified middle school teacher in Baltimore, Maryland, where he teaches science and computers.

Matt Thomas is taking business courses at Tompkins Cortland Community College. He hopes to transfer to a four-year college in two years.

Leana Horowitz graduated from Harvard University and then enrolled in the school for midwifery at Yale University. She is now a midwife in Washington State.

Nate Kipp is on his way back to college. "I've had two years to grow up," he says. "I like construction, but I want to focus on my education. I expect to major in engineering and math."

Sam Godin, who spent two years traveling with the band, Tribulations, is now a senior in the film department at Cornell University. That big break just never did come for the band, and the group decided to disband. "We could have stayed together, but some of us wanted to go back to school." He is writing music for soundtracks to be used in educational films. "Writing music for the movement of an amoeba has been quite a challenge," he says. He is considering the use of picture and sound together with computer programming. He still gets together with members of the band.

Trampas Strucker will attend Central Washington University in the fall of 1999. He plans to pursue an undergraduate degree in communications and a master's degree in elementary education. "I do a lot of public speaking all around the state of Washington—in elementary school I give talks on physical disabilities. And I talk to high school students about overcoming adversity, about believ-

"I've had two years to grow up. I like construction, but I want to focus on my education."

ing in yourself and your dreams." In 1998 Trampas was named one of
the ten outstanding members of AmeriCorps.

Chapter V

Internships: Unusual Opportunities, Unique Experiences

WASHING DISHES AT THE LOCAL EATERY OR RUNNING A CASH REGISTER MAY NOT BE WHAT YOU HAD IN MIND WHEN YOU DECIDED TO TAKE A BREAK FROM SCHOOL. Perhaps you are looking for something more meaty—something that will give you a broader understanding of a particular career path. Or maybe you want to explore two or three career possibilities all within a year's time. An internship might be just the ticket. What is an internship anyway? Is it just a lot of unpaid grunt work for some organization or business? Is an internship really different from a regular entry level job?

According to Jane G. Kendall, the former director of the National Society for Internships and Experiential Education, the following three things are what make an internship different from serving as a volunteer or working in an entry level job.

First, there is a partnership between the sponsor and the intern. In other words, the sponsor agrees to make sure the intern explores a wide range of tasks in a particular business or agency.

Second, there is a built-in intentional learning agenda for the intern. The intern (that's you) is expected to ask lots of questions, work hard, and come away from the experience with an understanding of a particular subject area or an organization or agency.

Finally, the intern goes through a continuous process of reflection, so that he or she can begin to understand both theory and actual practice during and after the experience. If you complete the internship as part of a school assignment, you will be asked to submit a written report about your experience, which may include a critique of your particular organization. Or, your sponsor may request a written report from you in order to help him or her make the next intern's experience better than, or at least as satisfying as, your experience. If you are doing an internship in connection with a school or college, you may be asked to present your project to scientists and other interns.

It is that careful mix of intentional learning and periodic reflection that is essential to a successful internship.

Ms. Kendall identifies the following options for internships:

1. Part-time or full-time

2. One month to two years

3. Paid or unpaid

4. Sponsored through an educational institution or arranged independently by a learner or host organization

5. Evaluated for academic credit or not credited

6. For learners from high school age through senior citizens

7. For a variety of goals such as academic, ethical, citizenship, career, and personal and social development

Internships also have definite advantages over an ordinary job or volunteer experience. They encourage the intern to do the following:

1. Acquire, apply, integrate, and evaluate a body of knowledge or the methodology of an academic discipline

2. Understand different cultures and environments

3. Acquire generic academic skills, e.g., identification of a problem, analysis, and synthesis

4. Develop and use an ethical perspective in complex situations

5. Develop knowledge and skills specific to a particular occupation, profession, or organizational setting

6. Acquire generic skills for effective adult life, e.g., oral communications, interpersonal interaction, coping with ambiguity, working in groups, setting goals, managing time—precisely the skills that will be important to you when you are out in the working world

7. Explore career options and gain documented work experience in a field that requires college-level knowledge and skills

So, how do you go about finding and setting up an internship with an agency or business? How does the internship actually work? How do you make sure to get the most out of the experience?

Before you begin to research internships, you ought to be aware that most, but not all, internships are unpaid. Some sponsoring organizations may even charge a fee. If your internship is in another city or state, you may have to pay your own transportation and/or housing costs. The sponsor must put out a lot of effort to make your internship experience successful and worthwhile. He or she assumes the role of a mentor, as well as your supervisor. There are, however, internships, particularly those that try to attract young people from disadvantaged backgrounds, that will provide a modest stipend or include housing and meals.

However, don't be put off by the fact that you or your parents may have to pay money for this experience. A successful internship can reap rich rewards, not the least of which may be the job you are looking for down the road.

Finding the internship that suits your particular needs may require research and ingenuity on your part. It helps if you know the area in which you'd like to work—in the sciences, on a newspaper, in a brokerage firm, at city hall, etc.

Your first stop ought to be your school guidance counselor or perhaps your favorite math or biology teacher. Most guidance counselors receive lots of information throughout the school year on various internship programs. They hardly ever have time to read through them all or figure out which ones are best. At worst, you will be handed a couple of packets of material, and it will be up to you to sort it out for yourself. At best, your counselor may know of someone who was an intern in a particular program. You can talk to that person yourself.

If you don't have any luck with your guidance office, head to your library and pick up the latest copy of *The National Directory of Internships,* put out by the National Society for Internships and Experiential Education. This book, which is updated every two years, lists thousands of internships in over 85 fields. If you focus on a particular field, you can browse through the book and find internships that accept high school students or high school graduates. Then you can follow up on some of the most promising ones on your own. There are numerous other guides on internships, including *Peterson's Internships 1999.* This one is updated every year.

Because these books become quickly outdated, it is best not to rely on them exclusively. Still, the books are a place to get started. Many current internships are also listed in magazines, such as *Art Search* for people interested in dance or theater. Other internships can be researched on the Web. In fact, there are some internships that have their application forms posted on the Web, but do be careful here. You want to make certain that the internship listed is truly reputable. Your teachers may also get special mailings on internships that they will pass on to interested students.

That's precisely what happened to Charlotte Schulze-Hewett. "I'm from North Iowa," she says. "I went to Benson High School, which now is a magnet school, but when I went there, there was a high dropout rate and lots of gangs. Only about 25 percent of the kids went on to college."

Charlotte says she's always been good in math, and "even though I wasn't interested that much in science, I took a lot of science in high school."

It was her physics teacher who mentioned the paid summer internships for Women in Science and Engineering at Iowa State University. Charlotte was the only person in her class to apply.

"It was a great opportunity for me. I always knew I would go to college. I was the oddball in my family—there are four of us kids. I'm the second oldest and always did a lot of child care, so I pretty much felt as if I were the oldest. My dad went to college but never did anything with his education."

Charlotte's placement was in a laboratory, where she worked on a program called the Neural Network. "It's a computer program that teaches the computer to think the way the brain learns. I was working on handwriting recognition. Back in 1991 I didn't know very much about computers except that I could type and do word processing. But I learned a lot that summer."

Krishna Athreya, coordinator of the Program for Women in Science and Engineering, says, "These are research internships. We take high school students (rising seniors) for a six-week period. At the end of the internship, the student writes a paper and presents a poster to groups of scientists and other interns. This paper or poster

"It was a great opportunity for me. I always knew I would go to college."

can lead to a publication. The internships are varied, but all are either in engineering or the sciences."

There are usually between 20 and 24 students taking part in the summer internships at Iowa State. They do not have to be residents of Iowa. Each intern gets a stipend of $1,250 for the six weeks. Out of that they have to pay for housing and food. Charlotte was very frugal with her money and actually came home with enough money to buy "a very cheap car that lasted most of my senior year."

The internship paid dividends when Charlotte decided on her college major and college. She applied to Iowa State and was offered a package of small scholarships. "I also have some student loans—about $10,000 worth, now that I've graduated. Before I started college, I thought $10,000 was a lot of debt. But now that I see what kinds of jobs I can get with my degree in chemical engineering, I realize that is really a small amount of money."

Charlotte's success has inspired both her older sister and her mother to enroll in a community college. A 1996 graduate of Iowa State, Charlotte has recently married a fellow student who is finishing up his degree. "So I'll be working for a year before going on to graduate school. This summer I will be working with Dr. Derrick Rollins, who does research in chemical engineering and statistics. My job will be to train the summer interns. So I've come full circle."

The opportunity to work in a laboratory with a research scientist also fascinated Michelle Stewart. She had always been torn between her two loves—music and science. All through high school she'd concentrated on music, but in her junior year she applied for an internship at The Jackson Laboratory in Bar Harbor, Maine. This lab has ties with the University of Maine and other colleges and laboratories that conduct research in mammalian genetics. She especially liked the idea that both high school and college students interned there.

Robert Shea, program manager for the training and education office, says that each student is sponsored by a member of the research staff. "A mentor relationship is established between the student and the researcher." The intern is directly involved in the mentor's research.

Michelle was amazed at how much information she absorbed in a short period of time. "I didn't have an extensive background in biology. I had my basics, but by the end of the summer, when I spoke about my work to the other students in a seminar, I kind of stopped and listened to myself. I was shocked. I had to memorize a lot of stuff; I had to have a working knowledge of terms. My sponsor worked closely with me, and he did a good job of imparting knowledge and inspiring scientific curiosity. It was all so fascinating."

Of course, landing an internship at Iowa State University or at The Jackson Lab is very competitive. "We look for students who have a deep interest and commitment in science. We want to make sure that the student will benefit most from the experience," says Krishna Athreya. "If we have a student from a small high school where they are limited in what they can provide to a student who is passionate in her field, that student would rank higher than a student from a very large high school with many facilities."

The interns at The Jackson Lab are chosen directly by the scientists, with the approval of the intern office, says Mr. Shea. "The staff looks for students who have demonstrated well-above-average academic ability, and perhaps most of all, a hunger for the opportunity to do research. They look for those who enjoy the process of discovery and have a genuine interest in the research process, rather than a student who is applying in order to make his or her college application look good." For high school students, there is a fee of $2,500 that covers room and board and tuition. College students are eligible for a National Science Foundation grant that covers this fee, plus a little extra.

But high school students may also apply for a scholarship that covers all fees but does not carry a stipend.

FINDING AN INTERNSHIP AT HOME

Tierra Reese had been taking every free program offered to children at The Nature Museum of Chicago Academy of Sciences since she was a little kid. By the time she was in ninth grade at Lindblom Technical High School, she was ready to move up to the Science Scene internship program. "I had gone to so many of the programs over and over again that I knew the answers to all the questions," she says.

"So one day Laura Sabransky (the volunteer coordinator) asked me to join the Science Scene Program. Now I'm one of them—one of the teachers. I work with kids in fifth to eighth grade, doing projects on wetlands, experiments with the packets we developed. On other days I work in the museum making sure nobody gets hurt. Some days I'll bring up Fred and Macha, our snakes, or Charlie and Claire, our turtles. And I talk about the reptiles," Tierra says.

If she is stumped by a question, she asks one of the older, more experienced college student interns to help her out. "But then," she says, "After I'm done with my shift, I go to the library and study so I won't be stumped again." In addition to studying on her own, Tierra has the opportunity to take workshops given by college students.

"Now I'm one of them—one of the teachers."

Once Tierra completed a training program at the nature center, she discovered that she would be getting paid for her work—$4.35 an hour. She is able to take part in this program all throughout the school year and during the summer as well. She finds that by working at the museum, her grades at school have improved. "People around me are surprised that I know the answers so much of the time. But a lot of what I learn at the museum, I can use in my school work."

Many science museums in larger cities have volunteer/internship programs for high school students.

■ **Program for Women in Science and Engineering**
210 Lab of Mechanics
Iowa State University
Ames, IA 50011
Phone: 515/294-0966
E-mail: pwse@iastate.edu
Web site: http://www.iastate.edu/~pwse_info/
Note: Deadline for applications: February 28

■ **The Jackson Laboratory**
600 Main Street
Bar Harbor, ME 04609
Phone: 207/288-6250 (training and education office: summer
            student program) and 207/288-6051 (public informa-
            tion)
E-mail: training@jax.org
Web site: http://www.jax.org/
Note: Deadline for applications: the second Friday of February

■ **Chicago Academy of Sciences**
Laura Sabransky, Volunteer Coordinator
2060 North Clark Street
Chicago, IL 60614
Phone: 773/549-0606
E-mail: cas@chias.org
Web site: http://www.chias.org/
Note: Chicago Academy of Sciences is closed until fall, 1999

A SAMPLER OF INTERNSHIPS

Gloria Shepard didn't really know what she wanted to do when she finished high school back in Williamston, Michigan. But she knew she wanted to get "away from Michigan and all the things I already knew."

A perceptive guidance counselor suggested that Gloria check out an internship program in Worcester, Massachusetts, called Dynamy, Inc. This program provides high school graduates with a year-long series of internships in a great variety of areas of the working world, from nonprofits to government agencies to private "for profit" businesses. Students live in three- or four-person apartments in a building owned by Dynamy. Before starting their individual internships, all students take part in a strenuous Outward Bound program during the first couple of weeks after their arrival.

"My parents were really against this," Gloria says. "My mother thought I wouldn't be able to get into college, and my father thought it was just a bad idea." But to Gloria, it was the chance of a lifetime. Her application was so strong that she was offered a full scholarship to Dynamy. "I only had to pay for my travel expenses," she says. She had no trouble earning that money during the rest of her senior year.

In addition to the internship experience, Dynamy also provides the 40 students with advisors who help them settle in and offer support in selecting three internships out of 200. Advisors also help participants prepare their college applications for the following year, if they are college-bound.

It was the Outward Bound portion of the year that had a powerful impact on Gloria. She had to scale a 50-foot wall, jump 70 feet from a ledge onto a tree stump, and do many other things she never believed she was capable of doing. She also learned the importance of team work.

"It was such a confidence-inspiring experience," Gloria says. As a result, she decided that "nature was pretty important to me." When she enrolled in New College in Florida the following year, Gloria had already decided on a major in environmental studies.

Gloria's first internship was with a Massachusetts state senator who had offices in Worcester. At first she found her work "pretty boring." All she was doing was data entry on the computer. Her advisor suggested that she speak to her sponsor to let her know she wanted more variety and helped her figure out the best way to approach her supervisor. Almost immediately things got better. New responsibilities were heaped on her as she proved time and again that she was very organized and capable.

The most exciting opportunity came when she was called upon to organize a community-based day-long informational program.

"I organized a program for representatives of 25 state agencies to meet with some of the senator's really poor constituents so they'd know how to utilize these agencies. That meant that I sent out letters to both the agencies providing services and people who could use them. I called people on the phone and went door-to-door to let constituents know we were seriously interested in their participation."

The payoff for Gloria was the knowledge that she'd organized a very valuable program for the state senator's constituents. She also gained important organizing skills, as well as an understanding of the issues affecting people in the Worcester area.

"It [Outward Bound] was such a confidence-inspiring experience."

Gloria's self-confidence soared. "I learned how to say 'no,' and I learned when the sponsors have a right to ask you to do things."

A Fantastic Experience

Remember Chris Batt from Chapter I? He was at loose ends after his unsuccessful first year of college. "I was working for a while in a sporting goods store." He had this dream about working in television.

An academic advisor suggested Dynamy. Chris was able to enroll for the second half of the Dynamy experience. "The kids were very receptive to me," Chris says. And since he came in with several other midyear students, they all took part in the Outward Bound spring offering, which is really in the middle of winter. "We did cross-country skiing and dog sledding. I loved it. I'm an outdoors kind of guy."

Chris got to do his first internship at WGMC Channel 3 in Worcester. "I did everything. I went out on shoots, used the camera and got to do on-line news. The interns ran the news programs. Most other interns were from the colleges in Worcester. I got to know every aspect of television work. I even got to work on some big stories. It was an eye-opening experience. I had managed my high school TV station. But during the internship, I realized the risks of TV, the crazy hours you had to be willing to work. I saw what it would be like in television production. And I knew then that I didn't want this for a career."

"I even got to work on some big stories. It was an eye-opening experience."

His second internship was with an engineering firm in nearby Concord. "I wanted to learn more about rowing. I'd been involved with crew and physical education all my life. This internship gave me hands-on experience and a lot of responsibility." The firm Chris was placed with builds and designs boats for racing. "I learned what it takes to build rowing boats, kayaks, and even the oars. This firm does the Olympic kayaks and the shells. This was a fantastic experience. I learned more about rowing—every aspect of it."

Although Chris tried another semester of college after Dynamy, he still wasn't happy there. But it was this second internship that helped him land a job he loves. "Now I'm a sales rep for an hydraulic company. And the engineering internship helped me enormously—especially in understanding how things work. I love what I'm doing now, and I'm still coaching crew at the Wilmington Rowing Club."

Not all students do as well as Chris and Gloria, admits David Rynick, who has been the director of Dynamy for several years. "Occasionally students do get fired from their internships. We meet with the student and the sponsor to find out why it happened. And sometimes we do ask people to leave the program. The kids need to be actively engaged. We don't call kids up on the phone and say, 'get to work.' If they get fired from two internships, they are out of the program."

Most recently, Dynamy has instituted a college credit option through Clark University. Rynick teaches a seminar once a week to those interns who are looking for college credit. A student can earn 12 credits by successfully completing the seminars along with three internships over the year.

The kind of person who does well in the Dynamy program, notes Rynick, "is one who wants to get involved in his or her education. These are risk-takers. They want to take the bull by the

> "I learned what it takes to build rowing boats, kayaks, and even the oars."

horns. This program is what students make of it. It takes a lot of initiative and desire. Once a student has taken part in the program, he or she may say, 'gee, maybe I should go on to school.'"

There is a wide mix of students. This is something that greatly appealed to Chris. "It was a good experience to live with kids who might have a different belief system than you. You can talk about a lot of things."

Some kids have a hard time being on their own. But Chris grew to like this part of the experience. "When I lived at home I never worried about what I spent." He knew his parents would always pick up his bills.

At Dynamy, Chris was responsible for buying his own food and paying all his own phone bills. He and the other students had to do this on $55 a week. "I actually learned to live on a budget," he says.

The cost for attending Dynamy for the year 1999-2000 is $10,250, plus $3,600 to cover the apartment rent. Parents are asked to deposit an additional $2,100 with Dynamy which is doled out in weekly increments to cover food, phone, and other living expenses." It helps students learn to budget their money," says David Rynick.

■ **Dynamy Inc.**
27 Sever Street
Worcester, MA 01608
Phone: 508/755-2571
E-mail: dynamy@nesc.org
Web site: http://www.ecotarium.org/~dynamy/

IT PAYS TO BE CAREFUL IN CHOOSING YOUR INTERNSHIP

How can you know for sure that the internship program you've chosen is going to be legitimate? How do you know it's right for you? Sometimes programs that have been around for some time turn out to be less than satisfactory.

This happened to Dara Silverman. Dara has been involved in social action activities ever since she can remember. She took part in antiviolence education while still in high school. She was trained as a mediator through the Dispute Resolution Center. Once she enrolled at Bard College in New York state, she became a sociology major with a concentration in gender studies. During her second year at Bard she went to the career and development center to look over the large number of internship possibilities. When she came upon an organization that was billed as a clearinghouse on marital and date rape, she became very excited. "I knew I wanted to do an internship that was involved with women's issues. I'd been involved with the Ithaca Rape Crisis Center when I was in high school. So it was natural for me to want to expand my education in this area. I figured it would lead me into crisis counseling."

Dara had read about this particular organization in "a bunch of different books." And then she phoned the director of the organization out in her home in California. But "when I got there, it was a little more than I'd bargained for."

"I knew I wanted to do an internship that was involved with women's issues."

For one thing, the organization operated out of the director's home. "And she had allergies, so everyone had to change their clothes when they got there and cover their hair and heads with 'shmattes' (rags). And she had all this cast-off clothing—pink pants suits that she made people put on, for example. I never had an experience like this. It was so unorganized. There were people everywhere. She had dozens of interns coming from all over the country."

Dara wound up organizing the files on a high-profile rape case. There were clippings from different press services about the trial, and it was very interesting. "But there really wasn't any space for me to do this, so I would sit on the floor next to a sliding glass door, which didn't shut all the way. And it was raining almost the entire month (this was January in San Francisco). There was a vent on the other side of the room that was blowing up hot air. So I was cold on one side and hot on the other."

Despite all of these inconveniences, Dara completed her task and ended up writing two different papers on the trial. "The director didn't have money to pay the interns, so I stayed with friends in the Berkeley area. And I did get to meet interns from almost every part of the country—from Florida, Utah, New York state. Many interns would arrive and leave very quickly once they saw this place."

> "I never had an experience like this. It was so unorganized."

So how did this organization manage to attract so many interns? According to Dara, the director has a national reputation because she "was very instrumental in getting marital rape laws on the books in the '70s and '80s." And while she doesn't get grant money to run her operation, which is also supposed to do rape crisis counseling, her reputation grows because she lectures all around the country at colleges and universities. "She has good credentials," says Dara. "But she has a million different things going on at once, and her home isn't a very well-constructed place to work in."

In hindsight, Dara thinks that she would have been wise to "get in touch with other organizations in that area that did antirape work to find out their opinion of this organization. And it would have been useful to talk to other interns. When I returned, all these people at Bard came up to me and said, 'Oh, I heard that you did an internship there.' So I was able to say, 'well, if you don't mind working in the midst of chaos, then you can do it. But if you want an organized experience, don't go there.' "

A word to the wise from a much wiser intern:

1. Don't get carried away by the reputation of the agency or organization. Before you agree to become an intern, get a written description of the work you will be expected to do.

2. Especially if you will be traveling a great distance to do your work, check with other organizations in the same city to find out what they think about the one you've chosen.

3. Talk to at least two people who have done the internship—more than two if you get conflicting reports.

4. If you do wind up in a difficult situation, you do have choices. You can quit and try to find another organization in the same area, or you can quit and go back home. Or you can, as Dara did, find something interesting to work on and get the most possible out of the experience.

Other Considerations

1. Does this internship program offer any special privileges or benefits?

2. Can this agency assist you in finding housing while you are there?

3. Can this agency assist you in finding a job?

4. Is there insurance to cover interns?

5. Will you be meeting other interns?

6. Are there special programs just for the interns?

7. What kind of supervision does the internship provide?

Chapter VI

How To Change The World During Your Summer Vacation

"THE WEIRDEST THING I EVER ATE," SAYS DAN ELSBERG, "WAS ARMADILLO. And the funny thing was that the armadillo was walking around the backyard that afternoon, when suddenly this guy pulls out his pistol and shoots the thing. And the next thing we knew, it wound up on the table. Cooked, of course."

That was during the summer after Dan's junior year in high school. He was in a tiny village in Paraguay with three other American high school students. They had joined up with a program called Amigos de las Americas—Friends of the Americas. And their mission was to spend eight weeks on an immunization project.

"My job was to give shots to children: measles, mumps, whooping cough, rubella, tetanus. And also I administered liquid polio vaccine." There were other tasks, as well. "We'd go into the school and give out toothbrushes and teach kids how to brush their teeth, and give mini-lectures in the church or school, and leave information with the teachers on the importance of the immunizations."

Dan's living accommodations were something less than spartan but more luxurious than all but three or four of the 200 families in the village of Encarnaca. Dan and the other male member of this intrepid quartet were housed in the home of the brother of the town doctor. The two girls lived at the new clinic. What set them apart was that both the house and clinic had glass windows, and the outdoor latrines were enclosed.

While most of the villagers appreciated the work Dan and the other kids were doing—indeed, Amigos only goes into communities that request them—sometimes there were quarrels among the elders. In return for the services provided by Amigos, the town agrees to feed and house the students. "Some of the community people thought that my hosts were embezzling the food money. I never found out if this was true," says Dan. But it was decided that the students would eat at a local restaurant. And at the end of their stay, the restaurant owner complained that he hadn't been paid. "So it fell to us when we were dispensing the polio vaccine to ask the villagers if they had paid their share." This made Dan very uncomfortable. "That wasn't supposed to happen."

But most of the experience was excellent. Even though some people were wary of the North American medicine, others would come up to Dan and say how much they appreciated their work. "One father said, 'I had eleven kids and four of them died of measles. I am so glad that you are here.'"

"One father said, 'I had eleven kids and four of them died of measles. I am so glad that you are here.'"

There were other rewards, including learning about another culture. Dan found the people in the village were "responsible for themselves, and had a great sense of community. Time is different from our time. What I saw in Latin America is that it is a great burden to feed four people. The hardest thing for me was coming back home. There was such culture shock. We have so much, and I would think, why do I need it all? I love having my stereo and computer and video games, but I really don't need these." Fortunately, Amigos had prepared the volunteers for these feelings and had suggested ways to cope. A big plus was that Dan's Spanish improved so much, that when he went to college a year later, he signed up for a Spanish literature course where the reading and discussions were all in Spanish. "There is no way I could have done that with just two years of high school Spanish."

*   *   *

Are you someone who thinks the world is pretty messed up, and there isn't much you can do about it? Well, you're partly right. There's a lot that needs to be done to make the world a better place.

The good news is, it isn't your fault. You never asked to be born into this world. To tell the truth, neither did anybody else. In fact, the world has always been somewhat of a mess.

The bad news is, this is the only world we have (as far as we know), and your generation is stuck with the job of figuring out how to make things better. Actually, every generation gets stuck with that task, and some do a better job than others. If you are one of the people who wants to create a better world, that is good news, indeed. There are many ways you can do your part.

While it may seem far fetched that an ordinary 18-year-old can make a contribution to saving the environment, right an injustice, create a better place for the homeless, or feed the hungry, there really are things a young

"This is the only world we have, and your generation is stuck with the job of figuring out how to make things better."

person can do to make the world a little better. Umm, no, you don't have to become president of the United States, and you don't have to be the first person to find a cure for AIDS or cancer. Nor do you have to be the one to plug the hole in the ozone layer. You can save those big ticket items for another time—or leave it for your kid brother or sister.

You can, however, commit a block of time to community service in your home town, your state, another part of the country, or in a foreign country. You can do this for three or four weeks over the summer, or take six months or an entire year after you finish high school to help improve life in one corner of the world. (You'll find year-long projects sprinkled throughout other chapters.)

The astonishing thing is that while you are doing something for someone else, the people you are working with are doing something positive for you. What you get back will be different for each of you.

Before you take time out for community service, you need to figure out :

- *Do you prefer a community group, a religious organization, or a government (city, county, state, or federal) agency?*

- *How much time do you have to give to a project—a couple of weeks in the summer, an entire summer, a semester, or a year?*

- *Must you earn money, or can you participate in a project that requires a fee for travel and living expenses?*

- *Would you be more comfortable in a structured environment where your work is laid out for you each day, or are you a self-starter who can be comfortable figuring out things on your own?*

Don't be put off by the cost of a program. According to Gideon Levenberg, longtime social activist and project administrator in Guatemala with Guatemala Partners, "Many students who do community service in Latin America have had extraordinary experiences volunteering with organizations that charge fees.

"Sometimes these programs cost the volunteer money. At first it sounds like a lot of money, especially if there is airfare involved. But that shouldn't put you off. You can save for it by working after school or during vacations. Also many of the organizations will help you with fundraising ideas, and sometimes there are partial scholarships. Think of it as an investment. You will get to learn a new language if you go to a foreign country. It is a new kind of living experience, and you will be making a contribution to the community. This kind of activity will also help you get into college or will help you get a job. Companies like to hire people who get involved in community service."

HOW LEARNING A NEW LANGUAGE CHANGED HIS LIFE

"Actually," Gideon admits, "I was always the worst student in my high school Spanish class. Even my teacher finally gave up and stopped asking me questions in class." But through after-school volunteer work with Latino immigrants, Gideon developed a deep interest in Latin American culture and politics. He knew that if he wanted to continue his education in Latin America and eventually land a job, he'd have to conquer this language barrier.

The summer after he graduated high school, some friends told Gideon about a private language school in Guatemala that they had gone to. Gideon jumped at the chance. He worked at a variety of temporary jobs to save some money and asked his parents to help out with the airfare. Gideon spent a total of eight weeks studying in private classes and living with a Guatemalan family, and another three weeks traveling the countryside. By the time he returned home, he was conversationally fluent.

"I was amazed at how fast I started learning the language once I was immersed in the culture," says Gideon. "Instead of testing you for all the words you don't know, like they do in the U.S., people down there are very excited that you are making the effort to communicate with them."

Gideon majored in Latin American Studies in college and later began working for Latin American focused non-profit groups. He credits this first experience with giving him the tools and inspiration for the career that followed.

"Studying in one of the private language schools in Guatemala is a great opportunity to immerse yourself in a language and a fascinating culture. And by doing this over a summer, you haven't locked yourself into a long-term program. It also gives you a chance to be more than a tourist."

Gideon notes that since the end of Central America's civil wars, Guatemala has become a major center for private language schools and tourism. Most of the schools offer the same basic program: five hours a day of one-on-one private instruction for five days a week, full room and board with a local family, opportunities to get involved in volunteer work, visits to

"I was amazed at how fast I started learning the language once I was immersed in the culture."

nearby Mayan villages and archeological sites, and after-school lectures and videos. The cost is somewhere between $100 and 150 per week, including classes, and room and board; it may be higher during peak summer months. Gideon warns that the quality of teachers varies. So be sure to ask for the names and phone numbers of two or three recent former students. And once you are there, don't be afraid to insist on getting an experienced teacher.

With a little effort most language schools can be found on the World Wide Web. A good source for schools in Guatemala is:

http://www.worldwide.edu/ci/guatemala/fguatemala.html

■ **Academia Guatemalteca de Español (A.G.E.)**
23 Avenida "A" 4-66 Zona 3
Quetzaltenango, Guatemala
Phone: 011-502-767-7469
Email: cafenet.xela@quetzal.net   Subject: "Silvia Hurtado"

■ **Instituto Central America (I.C.A.)**
U.S. address: RR #2 Box 101
Stanton, NE 68779
Phone: 402/439-2943
Guatemala address: 1a Calle 16-93 Zona 1
09001 Quetzaltenango, Guatemala
Phone: 011-502-763-1871
Web site: http://www.c.net.gt/xela/ica/

With your newfound language skills, you can make a difference in the life of a single person, or a family experiencing hard times, or a whole community. You can make a difference to a little kid living in poverty in Paraguay or Mexico by helping the family to replace a dirt floor in their home with a cement one. (And while you are doing that, you can improve your Spanish faster than if you had taken a six-credit college course.) Perhaps you will wind up working in an immunization center in Poland or with refugees in Germany, Holland, or France. Upon your return to the U.S., you can dazzle and amaze your friends with your foreign language skills and your ability to order interesting foods in foreign restaurants! In your heart, however, you will know that you have accomplished something ordinary tourists never do.

You can help renovate a row house in Philadelphia or Baltimore for a family who has been living in a cramped apartment or in public housing. Imagine! Without any prior knowledge about carpentry, you can learn how to put up sheetrock, tile a bathroom, and paint a kitchen. Those are skills worth having.

You can work in an after-school program in the South Bronx or Brooklyn with children who are temporarily homeless because their apartments were found to have high contents of lead. If the great outdoors is what makes you happy, you can blaze new trails, fix up old ones, clear old brush, and clean up the environment for two weeks or two months.

SUMMER PROGRAMS FAR & NEAR

A Summer in South America

After Dan Elsberg, who hails from Potomac, Maryland, finished his first summer in Paraguay, he decided he'd try a second summer after his freshman year of college. This time he signed up for a four-week session in Ecuador. He and a small crew of volunteers set to work building latrines set into casatas (enclosures) for the villagers. He knew from personal experience how much it meant to people in a small village to have this amenity. Each casata had a cement floor and a proper toilet seat. Although the assignment was to build 30 casatas during the four-week period, there were many delays, and they completed just four of them. "I really think that four weeks is too short a period," says Dan. "I recommend six- or eight-week work periods."

Among the things that Dan particularly liked about Amigos was the way students are prepared for their projects. Before he went to South America on the first excursion, he was sent a notebook that included chapters on many different topics relevant to the work he would do. Once he knew he'd be working on the immunization project, he met several times with his family physician and his dentist to ask questions. He also was required to fly to Houston, Texas, for a weekend training session (where he learned to inoculate a lot of oranges before he was allowed to try it on human beings). All students who take this correspondence course are required to do this. (In some parts of the United States, Amigos may have former volunteers do the training.) Besides getting instructions on the proper way to give shots, they were also counseled on "how we volunteers come off to a town. We shouldn't come off like 'Hey! We're here to show you the way.'"

Amigos also works with volunteers on safety issues. "We were given explicit instructions in case of illness, accidents, or other emergencies," Dan says.

Amigos de las Americas Projects

Amigos de las Americas is privately funded and has been operating for over 30 years. It carries out programs in Mexico, Costa Rica, Paraguay, Ecuador, Dominican Republic, Honduras, Bolivia, and Brazil. The program cost is $3,000, including airfare. Students will also need pocket money. Amigos provides volunteers with ideas for fundraising. There are four-week projects (Mexico only), six-week projects, and eight-week sessions. Students work in groups of two or three or occasionally larger groups. Volunteers are placed with youth leaders and field staff, all of whom are veterans of the program. Amigos looks for people who are either entering the junior or senior year in high school or who have graduated. You will need a basic understanding of Spanish or Portuguese (for Brazil), which will definitely improve while you are in the program. Dan recommends at least a year of Spanish, and more is better.

■ **Amigos de las Americas**
5618 Star Lane
Houston, TX 77057
Phone: 800/231-7796
E-mail: info@amigoslink.org
Web site: http://www.amigoslink.org
Note: There is a $25 application fee.

TRY A SUMMER WORK CAMP

If you have been spending your vacations going to summer camp and are looking for a different kind of experience, you might want to consider a work camp. Some are offered by organizations affiliated with religious groups. Others are privately funded. A work camp may operate in the United States, South America, Canada, Africa, or Europe—anywhere in the world where there is a need.

Dana Vetriecin from Highland Park, New Jersey, is no stranger to community service. "It is," she says, "a part of my life. It is something I do throughout the school year." After completing her junior year of high school, Dana signed on with the American Jewish Society for Service (AJSS).

The American Jewish Society for Service (AJSS) has been in business since 1950 and is directed towards juniors and seniors in high school, ages 15-17. Only 48 students are admitted each year, and they are placed in one of three work sites in the United States for a six-week period over the summer.

Carl Brenner, director of AJSS, says, "We are invited into a community for a six-week period and work with whomever the host community wishes—underprivileged kids, the elderly, etc. The volunteers will do things such as put a new roof on someone's house, paint and fix up a home, help people actually build their homes, or run a day care facility or a summer camp."

De-Constructing Houses

The mission given to Dana's group was unique. She was sent to Presque Isle in Aroostook County in Maine. All of the houses along a section of the Aroostook River had been destroyed by floods and ice jams the year before. The town fathers had decided it was too dangerous for people to live along the river. At first they had planned to simply bulldoze the structures that were still standing and build a park, while resettling the dislocated families in another part of town. Instead the 16 volunteers, eight boys and eight girls, dismantled the houses piece by piece, carefully saving anything that might be usable—from bricks and floorboards to kitchen sinks and bathtubs, fixtures and siding. Everything usable was donated to a materials bank run by Catholic Charities. They, in turn, sold the materials very cheaply to people who needed them to make improvements in their homes or to use in the new ones they were building.

"Someone, for example, who had never had a bathtub could get one for very little money," Dana says.

The project had far-reaching results. It saved the county hundreds of dollars in demolition costs, leaving more money to relocate the displaced families. And dozens of families would now be able to renovate and rebuild their houses.

Over the six-week period, Dana says, "we took down two trailer homes, a barn, and a house." Their site director was a local contractor who "had connections with everyone. He introduced us to the mayor, the governor, and we had a newspaper story written about us."

■ Weekends Were for Fun

The volunteers worked a full five-day week, Monday through Friday, and on Friday nights they met for a Shabbat service (the traditional Jewish Sabbath begins at sundown Friday night), which they wrote themselves. On the weekends the group would decide the kinds of activities they preferred. All decisions were by majority rule. "We went to Quebec one weekend, and camping another," says Dana. Several times the townspeople hosted the students for cook-outs.

■ Who Signs Up for AJSS Work Camps?

"Most of the students come from the Reform Jewish movement primarily because we do not offer kosher meals, and we use the weekends for travel and recreation," says Carl Brenner. However, it is not necessary to belong to a temple or a synagogue. Students can apply directly to AJSS. "Typically, the students are housed in a school building or in a synagogue," Brenner says. Dana's group lived in a nearby college dormitory, and there were five students living in a room that is normally a two-person dorm room.

■ Good Advice from a Participant

"You have to be the kind of person who likes to work hard and can live in a group situation. This can sometimes be difficult," Dana says. "There are often fights which do get resolved, but not everyone can get along with everyone else. You do find your group, though. And you have to be open to change. You don't always know what you will be doing next, but it all works out. And you find your own group of friends. I didn't know anyone when I went there, and I managed to make five good friends."

■ **When To Apply**

The cost of this program is $2,500 plus airfare and spending money. Brenner says, "This is a great experience in terms of group dynamics. It is a place where kids can make friends for life, and it is an experience of giving of yourself to people less fortunate." He noted that he, himself, was once a volunteer at an AJSS work camp site.

■ **American Jewish Society for Service**
Room 1029, 15 East 26th Street
New York, NY 10010
Phone: 212/683-6178
Web site: http://www.ajss.org/
E-mail: info@ajss.org
Note: Only 48 students are accepted into the program each sum-
    mer. It tends to get filled by April.

A Challenging French Experience

Johanna Kuhn-Osius spent her summer in France through a nonprofit organization called Volunteers for Peace. This organization was begun shortly after World War I and sets up work camps in partnership with a variety of host organizations throughout the world. The American head-quarters is located in Belmont, Vermont.

Jennifer Brewer, one of three coordinators of the United States pro-gram, says that over 400 volunteers from the United States go overseas, and approximately 400 people from Europe come to the United States and Latin America each year. Although 80 percent of the vol-unteers are college students or older, Brewer notes that "we have several programs for high school students who are at least 15 years old. The countries that accept younger students into their programs are France, Germany, Turkey, and Russia." Brewer herself went to Russia on a VFP work camp when she was a teen. All volunteers pay their own trans-portation to the work camp site. They also pay $175 to cover room and board. The American students are divided up so that two or three

Americans are working with up to 14 volunteers from other countries. English is the language spoken, but it is a more intense experience if the students can speak the language of the host country.

■ Don't Believe Everything You Read in the Brochure

Johanna was sent to a work camp in Auvergne. "It was a very rural setting," she stresses. "There were 16 volunteers. We slept in two very large tents in a sheep meadow. There was one shower and two toilets for the 16 of us."

The sparse washing-up facilities and the tents were the least of the problems encountered by Johanna. "I thought from the description in the brochure that I would be working with a group of 16 kids, and there would be two from each of the many countries. Instead, it turned out there were twelve French kids, two Americans, one from Italy, and one from Turkey."

Although Volunteers said knowledge of the language of the host country wasn't necessary, it would have been very difficult if Johanna hadn't spoken French. The other American spoke only English. But on this site everyone spoke French. It wasn't the kind of French you learn in school.

"The twelve French kids were mostly from group homes or were in foster care," says Johanna. "I have to say that my French increased dramatically. I certainly learned a lot of slang. And it is very different from speaking French in a school setting when you speak in their country with people your own age. The kids speak very fast and use a lot of slang and street talk. I had a bit of a rough time with the French kids. Most of them were there because they couldn't afford to do other things for the summer. Work camps are an inexpensive way to spend a vacation."

■ The Quality of Each Work Camp Can Vary

Jennifer says up front that Volunteers for Peace is a very decentralized organization. "Some work camps are better organized than others. There are more than 800 programs to choose from, ranging from laying out a student equestrian center to social programs with the elderly, or refugees or children's day camps, to remodeling houses, to organic farming and street theater."

■ Doing Work That Is Useful

Despite the difficulties with some of the kids, Johanna enjoyed much of her adventure. It happened that the other American girl lives just twenty blocks from Johanna in Manhattan—and they have stayed in touch. Also the work itself was important. Next to the sheep meadow where the students were housed was a chateau, originally built during the early Middle Ages. The students were restoring and rebuilding it so that eventually it would become a vacation retreat for people who are differently abled. Johanna's group was the second one to work on the project, and there would be others after she left.

"To do this sort of work camp, you have to be very tolerant," says Johanna. You never know what will happen. We laid tiles in the kitchen of the chateau, put cement in cracks in the stone basin which, when it is all completed, will be used as a swimming pool. We laid bricks and dug rain ditches in the forest. Another work crew dug a duck pond, while the ducks and geese and other animals milled around. When it rained, we worked inside the chateau scraping and sanding floors, painting, and tiling."

The work week was Monday through Friday, with a half day on Friday. Bedtime was 11 p.m. This was strictly enforced because although the tents had electricity, it was controlled from the chateau, "and at 11 p.m., they would turn off the electricity. If you tried to use a flashlight, the beam would attract all the bugs."

■ **Roll with the Punches**

On weekends the students hiked in the forests, and on Bastille Day (July 14) they walked into the village for the celebration. "We walked and hiked everywhere because there was only one car for the 16 of us. I wouldn't want to hide the fact that this work camp was unstructured," Johanna says. "But if you know this beforehand you can deal with it. Volunteers for Peace is a very good program. They can't control the organizations overseas. I am the kind of person who doesn't need organization to have a good time, and I didn't need the security of other Americans. But some of the time it was rough. Many of the kids would talk about their lives, and some of them came from areas where there were gangs, and so forth.

"If you do Volunteers for Peace, you need to have an open attitude. Maybe the next tour will be different. (Yes, Jennifer intends to sign up for another VFP work camp—this time with an older group.) It all depends on the partnership organization and the particular group to which you get assigned. And I did get to meet real French people."

Volunteers for Peace publishes an annual directory every April giving a sketchy outline of the various programs. After a student registers, he or she will receive more detailed information.

■ **Volunteers for Peace**
43 Tiffany Road
Belmont, VT 05730-0202
Phone: 802/259-2759
Fax: 802/259-2522
E-mail: vfp@vfp.org
Web site: http://www.vfp.org/

COMMUNITY SERVICE RIGHT AT HOME

If you are fortunate enough to live in a community that has a youth employment service, you can kill two birds with one stone: earn money over the summer while contributing to your hometown. Don Nguyen of Ithaca, New York, worked with a crew of 23 other teens building a footbridge across a stream in a recreational area called Six Mile Creek in upstate New York. Unusually severe winter storms had washed away the old bridge, and heavy summer rains made the bridge project difficult. Yet, Don says, "I learned a lot of new stuff about how to use tools and I actually learned how to build a bridge—and I got paid, besides." Sometimes when he goes past that bridge on the way home from school, Don thinks about the experience. "I just can't believe I put in all that work. It was such a great project for 16- and 17-year-olds."

Rick Dietrich, who coordinates the summer work projects for the Ithaca Youth Bureau, said the bridge project was one of the most ambitious the bureau had undertaken. It was especially difficult because of the rain. One thing Dietrich stresses is that it wasn't always easy to get 24 kids to work together harmoniously, especially in a situation where they were often knee-deep in water and mud. "But adversity seemed to have its positive effect, too," he says. "We had hired 24 kids, thinking that at least half of them would drop out. But no one did."

The bureau puts more than 200 teens to work each summer on a variety of community service projects. The size of the work group varies from four to six times that number. One group of teens built a playground,

> "I actually learned how to build a bridge— and I got paid."

another a bus shelter. Another project involved grading a hiking trail, and still another involved a group of teens who created a huge mural on the outside wall of a city building. Many of these projects are funded by a partnership between city and county, and it is worth checking with your community to see if such summer programs exist. This program pays participants minimum wage.

- **Ithaca Youth Bureau**
  1 James L. Gibbs Drive
  Ithaca, NY 14850
  Phone: 607/273-8364

A FINAL WORD

All reputable work camps will publish a list of participants with addresses and phone numbers from the previous year. Before you sign on with a program, call a couple of people and ask questions. As is obvious from those whose stories appear in this chapter, you have to be prepared to work in a variety of unusual situations. It would appear that having a sense of humor, as well as a lot of mosquito repellent, is a great help. You can surf the Web to find many other summer programs that have a community service component. Or if you belong to a church or synagogue, check out community service opportunities within your religious organization. Be sure to ask to speak to at least three kids who have signed up with these organizations within the past year or two.

Chapter VII

Can I Become A Real Man Or Woman By Joining The Military?

A TELEVISION COMMERCIAL SHOWS A RECENT HIGH SCHOOL GRADUATE TELLING HIS DAD HE'S GOING TO JOIN THE ARMY AND LEARN ALL ABOUT COMPUTERS. "I'm proud of you, son," his father says. "Be All That You Can Be," the television blares. "Join the U.S. Army."

The U.S. Air Force ad shows a handsome officer putting on his flight helmet. As he jumps into a sleek F-14 fighter plane and revs up the engine, he waves to a beautiful girl. Then he flies off into the sunset. "Join the Air Force," you are urged. "Become a fighter pilot." A U.S. Navy recruiter comes to your school in his crisp dress uniform and extols the virtues of a naval career. "If you join the Navy, you'll see the world." And of course, the United States Marines are always "looking for a few good men." You could be one of them.

"Well," you may think, "perhaps I ought to consider a hitch in the military." After all, when you turn 18, if you are male, you are obligated to register for the draft, even though at this time there is no draft.

Perhaps your father, brother, uncle, aunt, grandfather, or other relative served in the military. You've heard them reminisce about the "good old days." They gloss over the bad parts and talk about the different countries they were sent to, the friends they made, the good times they had—and of fulfilling an obligation to their country. One of them may slap you on the back and say, "the Army really straightened me out." Or, "I learned discipline in the Navy."

Perhaps a relative went to college under the GI Bill or got an ROTC scholarship. Getting some money to pay for your college education by giving your country a couple of years of your life doesn't sound so bad. It may even turn out that a military career is really what you are looking for.

SOME GREAT FINANCIAL DEALS

There are numerous financial deals available to those who join the military.

1. Reserve Officers' Training Corps (ROTC) scholarships are sponsored by the U.S. Army, Navy, Air Force, and Marines in more than 300 colleges and universities. There are scholarships available for two, three, and four years. According to Lt. Colonel Michael Merola, who is in charge of ROTC at Cornell University, in return for serving eight years in either the Reserves or on active duty after college graduation, plus about ten hours of classroom and field training each week during your four years of college, you can apply for substantial financial aid. For each of the four years you attend college, you may be eligible for a scholarship worth $12,800, $9,000, or $5,000. You will also be given a stipend of $150 a month, $450 a semester for books, plus $400 a semester toward lab fees. If you are admitted to one of the 25 super-tier universities, such as Cornell or Syracuse University, you can also apply for a $20,000 scholarship. These are highly competitive. Over 30,000 students apply each year. If you win a scholarship and then drop out of ROTC, you will have to pay back the scholarship money but not the monthly stipend. "Very few people drop out of ROTC," says Colonel Merola.

2. If you join a branch of the military, and get it written into your contract at the time of your enlistment, you can become eligible for a four-year education absolutely free, plus living allowances, thanks to Uncle Sam. Of course, there are tough qualifying exams to pass. One Army recruiter said that often these scholarships go begging because so few people apply for them at the time of enlistment. Once you are through with your basic training, you will attend the college of your choice, and you can wear civilian clothes. However, upon college graduation, you will owe the military eight years of service. After some further training, you will have officer's rank.

3. The National Guard will help you out while you are in school, if you pledge six years worth of weekends and summers. You will get $190 a month in college benefits, plus $130 a month pay. In many states Guards get free tuition in public colleges.

4. If you enlist in the military before you go to college and agree to kick in $1,200 from your paycheck, the U.S. Army, Navy, Marines or Air Force will boost that amount by another $13,200. Upon an honorable discharge, you will be entitled to a tax-free monthly installment of $400 a month (for nine months) for four years of college.

5. While you are in the armed services, there are many opportunities for you to attend college where you are stationed. Some of these college courses are free, and others are 75 percent covered.

WAIT!

Before you rush down to your friendly recruitment office and sign up, do some serious investigating. Be absolutely certain that you know what you are getting yourself into. Trying to get out of the military, if you decide it doesn't suit you, isn't as simple as dropping a course you don't like. The military can be a sensible choice. But if you don't get all the facts before you enlist, you may wind up a very unhappy person for the next two or four years. People who have served in the military will tell you that your attitude will determine a great deal about your life in the service.

LOOK BEFORE YOU LEAP

Tim Ryan of Groton, New York, had been admitted to the University of Delaware when he was just 16 years old, but he wasn't very motivated to do well. "I did manage to maintain a 2.8 average, but to tell the truth, I didn't go to classes very much, and I decided I was wasting my time."

Tim came back home after his first year and bounced around at various jobs for the next couple of years. When he was 18 he took the Armed Services Vocational Aptitude Battery (ASVAB). "I've always been a good test taker, and I did real well on it."

The ASVAB is given at your local high school by a test administrator from the federal government. It is free, takes about three hours, and requires no preparation. It does not obligate you in any way to join the military. However, once you've taken it, you can be certain that you will be called by recruiters from all branches of the service—especially if you score high.

> "I didn't go to classes very much, and I decided I was wasting my time."

Tim recalls how much he liked to play war when he was a little kid. "But I didn't have any concept of what that was like. I thought it was all Hollywood World War II movies. All of the glory and none of the blood."

While Tim was thinking about this, he was called by an Air Force recruiter who told him his test scores were great. He told Tim that one of the good things about the Air Force is that "it builds character and discipline."

"And," Tim says, "I thought, boy! I could really use a shot of discipline in my life." And here was the Air Force offering him a lifeline. He signed up for four years.

Tim used the computer in the recruitment headquarters to look up the many specialties the Air Force offers. "I wanted to go into intelligence," he says. "But there were no openings."

The recruiter told Tim that there might be openings in six months. "So if you go in now under a 'general category,' with your test scores, I can almost assure you that you will get what you want."

> "I thought, boy!, I could really use a shot of discipline in my life."

Tim was swayed by what the recruiter said. He figured that with his year of college Russian and his great test scores, he, Tim Ryan, was just the man Air Force intelligence was looking for. So he signed his contract under something called "general category."

His contract didn't say anything about being trained for intelligence.

Did Tim do something foolish? Yes, indeed. He soon learned that without a guaranteed contract, he would never make it into intelligence training. What Uncle Sam was after was his body, not his mind.

HOW TO AVOID MISTAKES WHEN ENLISTING IN THE MILITARY

The time to avoid making mistakes is before you sign your contract.

1. Forget about all the movies and TV shows you've seen about World War II, the Korean War, Vietnam, or the Gulf War.

2. Remember that the advertisements for the military are just that—advertisements meant to get you to believe you can be trained for something very special right out of high school.

No high school graduate can become a pilot. The television commercial doesn't tell you that you have to be a college graduate in a technical field such as engineering to even be considered for flight school. Then you have to spend time being trained as an officer, plus 110 hours as a pilot. According to former New York State Veterans Counselor Harry DeLibero, only 10 percent of those who are admitted into flight school ever succeed.

Very few jobs in the military are actually transferable to civilian life. There isn't much call for someone who can help build a bomb. There isn't much call for someone who can drive a tank. Counselor DeLibero notes that, "The military is not a college. They are not going to train you for civilian work." Although it is true that every person who is discharged from the military has his job listed in a parallel civilian name, most of those are not appropriate. Fully 30 percent of the job titles have no civilian name.

Much of the enlistee's work will center around carrying a rifle, pulling guard duty, picking up cigarette butts, and mindless drudgery.

You have to remember the purpose of going into the military is to learn how to kill. "Don't," cautions DeLibero, "ever forget that."

3. If the commercial or booklet says you can "go into computers," find out just what that means. If you are not careful, you will wind up sweeping out the room where they keep the computers. It doesn't mean that the Army will train you top to bottom with everything you ever wanted to know about computers, unless it is specifically written into the contract you sign.

4. The only ad that is realistic is the one in which there are guys driving tanks. As a high school graduate, you can learn to drive a tank, if that's what you want to do. But you will not spend all of your time doing that. You will do a lot of "policing" the grounds.

5. Read your contract, and don't be prejudiced by the person talking to you. Recruiters are trained to talk with 17- and 18-year-olds. They know exactly what to say to make you feel very important—and they have a monthly quota to fill.

6. Do not sign anything right there in the recruiter's office. Take your time. Take the contract home and have at least one other adult person go over your contract with you. If it doesn't say exactly what you want it to say, DON'T SIGN IT. Go back to the recruiter's office with your notes, and get the contract changed. Then take the second version home with you and have a responsible person go over it with you.

7. You don't have to sign up until the area in which you are interested becomes available. It's fine to wait several months or even a year for a specialty that really suits you. In the meantime you can get yourself some technical skills, perhaps by signing up for a course or two at your local community college.

8. There are some definite advantages to joining the military as long as you have a clear idea of what you are getting. The best advice is to take yourself very, very seriously. It is going to be your life on the line. Every day for the next several years you will wake up and still be a member of the armed forces. Every day for the next several years, you run the risk of being sent to war. You owe it to yourself, and to the branch of the service you choose, to see that your special talents are used to the fullest.

Be Sure Your Contract Says What You Want It To Say

■ *The contract you sign is inviolate and immutable. You can't change it, regardless of what the recruiter says.*

■ *Unless they are preparing you for some specific job (say you are fluent in Serbo-Croatian or Chinese, or that you play the oboe), you will be an ordinary recruit.*

■ *If you are 18, have just finished high school, and have never signed a contract before, you are in a very vulnerable position.*

■ *If, after you have been trained for a specific job, that job isn't available, you will be offered a different job. You have the right to refuse it and leave the service with an honorable discharge. However, until your discharge comes through, you can be subjected to a lot of harassment. It may not be pleasant.*

CAREFUL RESEARCH PAYS OFF

Like Tim Ryan, Steve Yatko from Clark Summit, Pennsylvania, had always been interested in the military. "My father," says Steve, "is a civilian who works for the government." Steve always believed that serving his country in some capacity was in the cards for him. Steve dreamed of becoming a pilot. "I've wanted to fly ever since I was a baby," he says. In fact, he obtained his private pilot's license before he turned 16. Steve believes that the "military is the best place to get flight training. And after training, you can fly the world's best aircraft. I want to do that. All of my life, flying has been a constant."

But Steve had another reason for becoming a military man. "I was always a B student. My SAT scores were 1130. I looked upon myself as an average student. There are millions of people just like me and millions of people who are smarter than I." Steve knew that he'd have to do something outstanding in order to qualify for an ROTC scholarship.

At 16 Steve had put together a lot of things about himself: his assessment of his scholastic abilities; his desire to be of service to his country; his love of flying; his desire for a college education with a major in government. Then he talked to lots of people, both in the military and out. "I got a lot of opinions and ideas on different routes I might examine."

Steve decided the Navy had the most to offer him. He found a special Navy prep school called BOOST, designed specifically to train future naval officers. In order to get into BOOST, you must agree to join the Navy. "If you pass their very stiff courses in chemistry, calculus, physics, English, writing, and reading," Steve says, "you get a scholarship to an ROTC school or to the Naval Academy in Annapolis."

Steve took the ASVAB and did well enough to be admitted to BOOST. "All I had to do then was to enlist and join the Navy." Just after Steve celebrated his 17th birthday, he found himself 3,000 miles from home at boot camp in San Diego, California. He knew that if he flunked out of the BOOST program, he would owe the Navy seven years of active duty. And there is a 50 percent drop-out rate from BOOST.

But Steve did well in the program. He was admitted into the Naval Academy. But after a year, he felt he was not getting what he wanted out of Annapolis. BOOST had promised Steve (in writing) a college education either at the Academy or at a college with an ROTC program. He transferred to a college in upstate New York.

Steve had no guarantee that he would make it into flight school after graduation. "I think the only thing that is certain in life is death," he says. But he passed all of his tests and last heard was on his way to flight training.

THE COAST GUARD BECKONS

Remember Lucy Morris from Chapter I? She also had been in love with flying and had made flying the centerpiece of her life. Like Steve, she had gotten her private pilot's license while still in high school. She had even obtained her flight instructor's license a few years later but was looking for more challenges. "I would like to teach flying at a different level than what is taught at the little airports. I'm interested in the whole psychology of the human being as it relates to flying."

While Lucy was casting about for a way to move on, she says, "I woke up one morning and said, 'Coast Guard.' And I called up a recruiter and got information. I enjoy helping people, and I enjoy listening to people." It seemed to her that all the things she liked to do were things that were done in the Coast Guard. She liked the idea of helping people during natural disasters. "If I did that sort of thing on a volunteer basis, I'd have to take time off from my job. But as a Coast Guard member, I'd be getting paid for doing things that are important." She also liked the pay scale. "I guess it is around $900 a month, plus room and board. As someone who has always been extremely broke, I'm going to be very cautious with the money I earn. I've got a lot of student loans to pay off, and I'll try to use my money wisely."

There were several things that were worrisome to Lucy. "I spent a lot of time going over the time commitment in my mind—four years of active duty and four years of inactive service. It did scare me. But I talked to a lot of people and found that the general public image of the Coast Guard was very good. And that people who are in the Coast Guard are generally happy with what they do." Lucy also liked the fact that she has found virtually no discrimination against women in the Coast Guard. The one time an instructor made a comment about "all you guys," he immediately corrected himself. "I meant men and women," he said. The Coast Guard has accepted women since 1970.

IF YOU BECOME DISILLUSIONED

Even though Tim Ryan soon realized he'd made a mistake when he didn't sign up for a specific job, he decided to save his money and try to enjoy himself for the four years he was in the Air Force. His straightforward attitude and high spirits landed him a job in communications training. His job was to fly with a crew into an area to set up the advanced air bases. "In case of a war," he says, "we'd have to fly in and set up the communications system." Fortunately for Tim, there was no war during his years in the service.

For the first year and a half, Tim had a good time in the Air Force. By the end of his second year, "I just became more and more disillusioned." It wasn't anything definite. It was more a matter of observing some things that were happening to his friends when they got into trouble. Some of them received less than honorable discharges.

"A less than honorable discharge," says Counselor DeLibero, "is very serious. You can never go back in the service to reverse this. Any time you apply for a job, you may be asked if you have ever served in the military. When you answer 'yes,' a prospective employer may ask to see discharge papers. The unfortunate thing is," DeLibero says, "that if the young person never had gone into the service, he or she wouldn't have that prejudice against them. If, for example, your discharge says something like, 'inability to adapt to military life' because you didn't want to be there, or showed up late for inspection, you probably won't get the (civilian) job."

Tim had also done a lot of thinking about what he wanted to learn in college. He was anxious to get back to school. So he began a dialogue with his commander. He told him how strongly

"A less than honorable discharge is very serious."

he felt about getting out of the Air Force. This didn't please his commander, who was a career officer. Career personnel tend to see those who enlist for a short period of time, and who complain about the military life, as scoundrels and worse. Tim's commander sent him to see a psychiatrist. After some time, however, even his commander recognized that Tim was sincere in his desire to get out. Because there were many people who wished to get into the Air Force at that time, Tim was able to leave with an honorable discharge after two years.

If Tim had used his dissatisfaction as an excuse to get into trouble, he would have risked a less than honorable discharge, and the stain on his record would have followed him for the rest of his life.

Tim was fortunate. He had over $6,000 in his education fund, plus $2,500 in savings. And he didn't feel all that negative about his experience.

"If anyone ever asked me about going into the Air Force, I'd say, 'go ahead.' I would tell you to go for it." Among the things he remembers best are the friends he made and the cities he got to see. When Tim got out of the service, he enrolled at SUNY Cortland and graduated with a degree in philosophy.

LEARNING TO TAKE RESPONSIBILITY FOR HIMSELF

John Weeldreyer was 18 when he joined the Navy. He was one of those kids who just "floated through high school" not knowing what he wanted to do with himself. "I didn't have the money or the parental support at that time. And I was always blaming other people for what went wrong in my life. When I was in high school, I dropped out of everything if I didn't feel like doing stuff," he says. "I didn't know what I wanted to do—should I stay in Hickory (North Carolina) or go into the

Things to remember if you become disillusioned

■ *It is a very serious matter when you enlist in the military.*

■ *If you decide you don't want to stay in the military, or if you get into some sort of trouble, you will soon discover you are in a "legal process." The controls are all there, and the system is stacked against you.*

■ *If you do get into trouble, insist upon your right to an attorney. If the attorney provided doesn't help you, ask to see another one. That is your right.*

■ *Everything in the military requires that you sign papers. Do not sign any paper because someone tries to browbeat you. Keep careful notes of what your superior officers say and do to you.*

■ *From the time you are in the military, you are trained to do what you are told. But when you are in trouble, the only way you will get a fair hearing is by not signing any papers that waive your rights. Yelling foul after you are released from the service will not help if you have signed papers that give up your rights.*

military or go to college?" Since he didn't have the money for college, John took the ASVAB. He racked up a perfect score.

"The recruiters were all over me—the Marines, Air Force, and Army. For a while the Air Force looked like a possibility. But the openings in the Air Force were only in administrative programs." And he turned down the Army and the Marines "because I didn't want to get yelled at." When the Navy offered him a program in identification work—in the Signal Corps—John signed on. "I was given a lot of responsibility," he says.

And John learned "a lot about taking responsibility for myself. In the Navy, everything was up to me. There was no one to rescue me, and there is no second chance in a lot of situations. I learned that I was an adult with adult responsibilities."

John also took advantage of the educational possibilities the Navy offered. In addition to putting $1,200 into the GI Bill fund (which grew to $14,000+ upon his discharge), he started taking college courses while he was stationed in Norfolk, Virginia. Most people take only one course a semester. "I wound up going to classes four nights a week. The Navy paid for everything."

Although John was accepted into Annapolis and gave it serious consideration, just a few days before he was to be sworn in, he decided he wanted to go to a regular college. "I realized my heart wasn't in it." He felt that there was a downside to a long-term commitment to the military. "In the military, creativity isn't stressed. If you fulfill your job, you'll go far. But no one wants your opinion. The Navy is not a college. You do what they tell you to do."

At the end of his two-year enlistment, John left the Navy and went to Appalachian State (North Carolina) where he did a double major in psychology and business. One of the things John is especially proud of is the fact that he graduated from college just after he turned 22—basically the same time most of his high school friends graduated. Today John is an assistant manager in the loan department at a major bank in Raleigh. He is planning on going on to graduate school to earn an MBA. "Eventually, I'd like to run my own company. I want to be challenged.

"My advice to people who are thinking of joining the service is to check out all your options. Keep an open mind. Some people won't be able to take the pressure of military life. And frankly, if they had given me the option of getting out after six months, I would have taken it. But I'm glad that I had those two years in the Navy. It's a place where I grew up."

CHAPTER VIII

Early College Admission: A Wise Choice For Smart Kids?

DO YOU FEEL YOU ARE SIMPLY WASTING TIME IN HIGH SCHOOL? Are you the sort of person who gets your homework done in 15 minutes because the assignment is so easy? Have you ever had the experience of being out of school for a long period of time only to discover you hadn't missed much? Do you feel that your senior (or junior or even sophomore) year of high school is going to be boring instead of intellectually stimulating? Do you wish, more than anything, that you could be in college right now?

Lorin Dytel was determined to graduate from high school in Jericho, New York, when she was 16. She had a difficult time convincing her school to let her do this. She was the first person from her community to be accepted into The Johns Hopkins Center for Talented Youth (CTY) summer program. She'd been going there every summer since seventh grade and had taken so many advanced placement courses that her high school had nothing more to offer. "I liked it at CTY," she says. "I was really academically challenged and met other kids who liked the same things I did." Knowing that college level courses were so much more exciting compared to her high school courses convinced Lorin to complete her secondary education as soon as possible.

■ **Center for Talented Youth**
Institute for the Academic Advancement of Youth
Dr. Julian C. Stanley, Founder
The Johns Hopkins University
3400 North Charles Street
Baltimore, MD 21218
Phone: 410/516-0337
Fax: 410/516-0804
E-mail: iaay.programsinfo@jhu.edu
Web site: http://www.jhu.edu/~gifted/registration/

Of the five colleges Lorin applied to, she was accepted at two and chose to go to the University of Chicago. "I know that I didn't get into some of the other colleges because of my age, but being a younger student at Chicago doesn't really make a difference. Although," she concedes, "you might have more problems socially if you are a male. There are fewer females at Chicago so the social life for women is great."

Of course, Lorin had to limit her social activities because of the workload. "It really shocked me," she says. "Every weekday, except for Friday nights, I studied. It took me until the second quarter to get the hang of it. But I definitely liked the great conversations we had there. It was a lot better than in high school. College is a very different kind of life from high school."

Kimberly Carter of Edison, New Jersey, wasn't a super straight-A student in her high school. "But," she says, "I love to study things that interest me." The summer after her junior year, Kimberly attended Rutgers University Summer College for high school students. "I knew even before the summer was over that I didn't want to go back to high school. I was taking this course in archaeology, and we were doing some actual digging in an ancient Leni-Lenape settlement in Washington County. It was the most exciting thing I'd ever done."

When Kimberly spoke with the summer college advisor, she discovered that Rutgers offered an early admission option. She instantly applied.

Even though Kimberly's high school grades included a couple of Cs, recommendations from her summer college professors were very strong.

"My parents were definitely not happy about this," says Kimberly. "They figured they had one more year before they'd have to help me with college costs, and I had two other siblings still in college." So she offered to live at home and commute the short distance to the New Brunswick campus to save money. Rutgers offered her enough work-study opportunities to meet the modest tuition costs her first year. "I was just happy going to college," she says. "I didn't much care if I lived on campus or not."

EXPLORE YOUR OPTIONS

Perhaps cutting short your high school years and going to college early is right for you. If you do decide to explore this option, you will be among a very small minority of students. It will definitely be an uphill battle, since many high schools do not like to lose their top students, and colleges may be reluctant to accept you if you are under 17 years of age.

Dr. Julian C. Stanley, who pioneered the program for academically talented youth in the 1970s at The Johns Hopkins University, notes that while many colleges, including The Johns Hopkins University, accept younger students, they do not provide any special supports for them. And it can be very difficult for a 15- or 16-year-old living in a college dorm to adjust to the kind of college life a typical student of

"I was just happy going to college. I didn't much care if I lived on campus or not."

18 lives. "Often, he says, "the younger student who commutes to college has an easier time."

Many admissions directors are not anxious to accept younger students because they are aware that adjusting to college life can be a significant problem. They look for students who are achievement oriented and have something unusual to offer. And they prefer that younger students show that they have exhausted all of the options at their high school.

There are, however, a number of possibilities for students who are serious about moving on to college before they have completed high school. In addition to four-year colleges, community colleges should not be overlooked. In New York State, for example, any student who completes 24 credits at an accredited college in a degree-granting program will not only receive his or her high school diploma (from the home school) but will also have a full year of college credits. Many other states have similar arrangements, or they encourage early college students to take the GED (General Education Diploma) test after they complete a year in college.

Leela Steiner used her community college as a jumping-off place once she decided not to continue on in high school. She had gone to alternative public schools in Ithaca, New York, from the time she was in second grade. Her sophomore year of high school was spent in an alternative school in Teaneck, New Jersey. When she returned to Ithaca the following year, she didn't want to go to either the traditional or alternative high school. "I had already taken a couple of courses at Fairleigh Dickinson University. I'd taken advanced placement summer courses at Smith College, and I thought I could handle college," she says.

Leela was two months short of 16 when she enrolled in Tompkins Cortland Community College in Dryden, New York. She had decided on the community college route because she hadn't taken the SATs.

Happily, she found several other high school "dropouts" enrolled at the college that semester, and the four became close friends. But by the end of the first semester, she found the academics less challenging than she'd hoped. Nevertheless, it was time well spent. "The community college got me into the semester system and into taking finals."

She transferred to Ithaca College, which accepted her community college courses and didn't require that she take the SATs since she'd already proved she could do college work. At Ithaca College Leela discovered the courses were extremely rigorous. "I had very hard classes at Ithaca College because my dad (who was a professor there) had recommended the most high-powered teachers to me. I got into college before there were lots of requirements, but it turned out that because I was curious about things, I took a lot of what was later required."

But what if you don't want to be thrown into a sink-or-swim situation with all the other older college students? Well, there are a small, but growing number of colleges that do have special programs especially designed for the early college student. Three are private colleges. Others are public colleges, some of which are open only to in-state students. Others are open to all who qualify.

PRIVATE COLLEGES

Simon's Rock College of Bard

Simon's Rock College of Bard, located in Great Barrington, Massachusetts, was founded in 1968. It has a total student body of 350 and is the only liberal arts college in the United States designed solely for the early college student. Its entire freshman class is composed of students between the ages of 14 and 16. Students who complete the first two years are awarded an Associate of Arts degree. At that point they either transfer to another four-year college or reapply to complete the bachelor's degree at Simon's Rock.

Vice president and dean of the college Bernie Rogers says that it is important not to "simply admit students into a body in which they are a minority, without providing special services for them. We feel the best way to serve these (young) students is to specifically educate them among their peers. An adolescent who is intellectually capable of doing college work is still an adolescent emotionally. At Simon's Rock close attention is paid to the student's life outside the class. There are many more services available to Simon's Rock students than at traditional colleges, as well as a higher ratio of adult resident counselors."

Most recently Simon's Rock has begun a national talent search aimed at tenth graders whose "achievements merit the opportunity to attend Simon's Rock with a full scholarship." At the present time there are 30 full scholarships awarded each year under the Acceleration to Excellence fund. Tuition with room and board is currently $28,650. There are numerous partial and full scholarships available at Simon's Rock.

PEG at Mary Baldwin College

In 1984 the all-women's Mary Baldwin College in Staunton, Virginia, established PEG (Program for the Exceptionally Gifted). Students who are accepted into the program must have completed at least eighth grade. For the first two years the girls live in separate dormitories with resident counselors who provide a lot of emotional support. There are programs tailored to the special emotional and social needs of young college students. All college courses are taken with the traditional Mary Baldwin students. Tuition and fees for the PEG program are $21,365. Approximately 70 percent of the students receive need-based assistance.

The Clarkson School

The Clarkson School was founded in 1971 specifically for talented young people interested in the sciences. It offers a special one-year "bridge" program to students who have finished eleventh grade (and other grades in special cases) and are truly ready for the challenge of college work.

Gary F. Kelly, headmaster at Clarkson, says, "We seek students who have done well in their present setting and who have scored high on the SATs. Our average math score is 700 (out of a possible 800). Average verbal score is 600. In addition, we look for the accelerated high school student who has been recommended by the people who know the student best." Basically, Clarkson students have taken all the advanced placement courses offered by their high schools and have enhanced their studies at such places as The Johns Hopkins Center for Talented Youth, Northwestern University, Duke University, and the University of North Carolina.

The 70 to 100 or so students admitted to The Clarkson School take their classes with the regular Clarkson University students. However, they live in separate housing apart from the other students. ("Actually," says one "schoolie," "our housing is much better than freshman housing.") Each house accommodates eight to ten students plus a resident counselor. All enjoy once-a-week "family style" dinners with Clarkson faculty and staff and get to go on special trips. Most Clarkson School students transfer to more prestigious universities after their "bridge" year, although a few opt to continue at Clarkson University. Tuition with room, board, and other fees at The Clarkson School is $26,836. The average scholarship is $7,525, but scholarships range from as little as $1,000 all the way up to $17,000.

■ **Simon's Rock College of Bard**
84 Alford Road
Great Barrington, MA 01230-9702
Brian Hopewell, Admissions Director
Phone: 413/528-0771
E-mail: admit@simons-rock.edu
Web site: http://www.simons-rock.edu/

■ **PEG at Mary Baldwin College**
Staunton, VA 24401
Dr. Celeste Rhodes, Director
Phone: 540/887-7039
Fax: 540/887-7187
E-mail: peg@cit.mbc.edu
Web site:
        http://www.mbc.edu/academic/undergraduate/peg/ind
        ex.html

■ **The Clarkson School**
Clarkson University
Grant Thatcher, Director of Admissions and Financial Aid
PO Box 5650
Potsdam, NY 13699-5650
Phone: 800/574-4425
E-mail: tcs@clarkson.edu
Web site: http://www.clarkson.edu/~tcs/

STATE-SUPPORTED SCHOOLS

Just a handful of states have recognized the need to encourage their brightest students, especially those from communities where there are limited educational resources. Texas has instituted two early college options. The program at Lamar University in Beaumont, Texas, known as Texas Academy of Leadership in the Humanities (TALH), began in 1993 and has grown from just 35 students the first year to 150 entering in the fall of 1996. The Texas Academy of Mathematics and Science (TAMS) at the University of North Texas in Denton has been accepting students since 1987 and each year admits 200 students. Both TAMS and TALH are open only to residents of Texas, and both are two-year programs. The emphasis in the TALH program is on development of leadership skills and liberal arts. The TAMS program focuses primarily on math and science. Students at TAMS pay $3,800 for room and board. Tuition, books, and lab fees are free. Tuition, room, and board at TALH is $5,300. Scholarships are available.

Both programs recruit students who have completed tenth grade.

In 1995 the state of Georgia chartered the Advanced Academy of Georgia at The State University of West Georgia located in Carrollton, about 50 miles outside of Atlanta. This program, which began with just 21 students, will expand as the need increases. Unlike the Texas programs, it is open to both in-state and out-of-state students who have completed the tenth or eleventh grade. Room, board, and other student fees for Georgia residents are less than $6,000. They pay no tuition. Out-of-state students pay approximately $10,500.

The state of Georgia has also chartered the Georgia Academy of Mathematics, Engineering & Science (GAMES) at Middle Georgia College, located in Cochran, Georgia. GAMES has been designed to meet the needs of gifted high school juniors and seniors who have exceptional ability and interest in engineering, mathematics, science, computers, and allied health fields. And GAMES, like the Advanced Academy of Georgia, is open to both in-state and out-of-state students. The program had 50 students for the 1998-99 school year. The annual cost for GAMES is $5,000 for Georgia residents; out-of-state students pay approximately $8,500 per year. Financial aid is available.

There are stiff entrance requirements for each of these state-funded early college programs.

- **Texas Academy of Mathematics & Science**
University of North Texas
PO Box 305309
Denton, TX 76203-5309
Phone: 940/565-3971
E-mail: admissions@tams.unt.edu
Web site: http://www.tams.unt.edu/

- **Texas Academy of Leadership in the Humanities (TALH)**
Lamar University
PO Box 10034
Beaumont, TX 77710
Phone: 409/880-2994 or 2995
Fax: 409/880-8384
Web site: http://hal.lamar.edu/~talh/

- **The Advanced Academy of Georgia**
The State University of West Georgia
Carrollton, GA 30118
Phone: 770/836-6445
E-mail: dbooth@sun.cc.westga.edu
Web site: http://www.westga.edu/~reslife/academy/acad.html

- **The Georgia Academy of Math, Engineering & Science (GAMES)**
Middle Georgia College
1100 Second Street, SE
Cochran, GA 31014-1599
Phone (admissions office): 912/934-3103
E-mail: games@warrior.mgc.peachnet.edu
Web site: http://www.mgc.peachnet.edu/

There are a sprinkling of other commuter-based programs through-out the country. Among these are the Early Entrance Program at California State University in Los Angeles, which accepts students who are at least 11 years old but not older than 15-1/2, and the Early Entrance Program at the University of Washington in Seattle, Washington, which accepts students under the age of 15.

- **Early Entrance Program**
  California State University at Los Angeles
  5151 State University Drive
  Los Angeles, CA 90032-8227
  Phone: 323/343-2287
  Fax: 323/343-2281
  E-mail: rmaddox@csla.edu
  Web site: http://www.calstatela.edu/

- **Halbert Robinson Center for the Study of Capable Youth**
  University of Washington
  Guthrie Annex II
  Box 351630
  Seattle, WA 98195-1630
  Phone: 206/543-4160
  Fax: 206/685-3890
  E-mail: cscy@u.washington.edu.
  Web site: http://weber.u.washington.edu/~cscy/

WHO GOES TO COLLEGE EARLY AND WHY

Students go to college early for a variety of reasons. Not all of them are sound ones. So it's important to take a close look at your real motives before you decide to opt out of high school. Go back to your self-assessment test and review that picture of yourself.

As you read through the stories of those who have gone to college early, see if you share some of their goals and aspirations. Those who are successful in college have an overriding desire to learn. They are emotionally ready for the challenge and will work hard to prove they made the right choice. Many of those who chose to leave high school early didn't have a large group of friends and therefore didn't mind striking out on their own. Others were popular with their high school classmates but were eager to accept new and difficult challenges. Says Kimberly, "Studying is a solitary activity. If you think spending five hours a night in the library is fun, then going to college early is for you. People who do well academically have to put in hours of studying by themselves. It's a natural extension of yourself."

Another student warns, "If your sole reason is to party and get away from your parents, going to college early would be a waste of your time."

People who choose to go to college early come from a variety of backgrounds. Some are from very small rural high schools, where they feel totally out of sync with the rest of the students. Others have already taken college courses, either during summer vacations or as part of their high school curriculum, and feel, as Leela did, that they can handle a full college load. Some are straight-A students and have been labeled "gifted and talented" by their school districts. Others are doing rather ordinary work in high school because they haven't been challenged, but often they study subjects that interest them on their own.

Gifted and Talented

Anne Byford grew up in Greenville, South Carolina, and was about to enter ninth grade when she learned about the PEG program at Mary Baldwin College. "I was just 14, and I would have had to go to a very poor school," she says. "It turned out that PEG was just getting started, and I was one of 11 students. Eight of us completed that first year, and we all either graduated from Mary Baldwin or from some other college."

> "I loved PEG. I loved everything about it—the classes, the other students, the staff."

"I loved PEG. I loved everything about it—he classes, the other students, the staff. I was coming from a bad situation, and this (PEG) was ideal. I had to work hard, but nothing was overly difficult. I did have to struggle with English, but that's because English isn't my strong suit. I always knew I'd major in biology."

The only downside of Anne's experience at Mary Baldwin College was that when she graduated with a bachelor's degree in biology, she was barely 18. "And I couldn't even celebrate with a (traditional alcoholic) drink!" Other than that, age was not an issue for Anne.

Anne was accepted to all four of the graduate schools to which she applied and chose Baylor College of Medicine "because they gave me a very decent stipend," she says. "And I knew I'd have to live completely on my stipend." She decided to do a Ph.D. in genetics with a clinical component. But she soon learned that while genetics fascinated her, she didn't want to do "human-based research."

The only problems Anne encountered at Baylor because of her age were "when my fellow students found out I was only 18, there was a lot of jaw-dropping, but then we just got on with it. Well, my thesis advisor had a little trouble with the age factor. He had a son exactly my age and had trouble making that leap.

"Early college worked fine for me. It was a lifeline. But it is the sort of experience that is either exactly right for you, or it can be a disaster. One of the things I liked about PEG is that I had people around me who were sort of like me. I wasn't the only one who was weird."

Placed in the Wrong High School

Rodney Christopher, an African American student from the Crown

"One of the things I liked about PEG is that I had people around me who were sort of like me."

Heights section of Brooklyn, New York, didn't make it into either of his two first-choice high schools. He did get into Brooklyn Technical High School. Most high schools in New York City have a special focus, and students have to pass exams in order to get into the better ones. Through a computer foul-up, Rodney's application for his first choice was voided, so he decided to make the best of it at his third choice.

"I did really well there," he says. "And I didn't hate it. Yet, I didn't know what I wanted to do. I just knew that this wasn't it." By the end of his sophomore year, Rodney was ranked first in his class of 1,200. He'd taken his PSATs, and shortly after his scores were out, he received a brochure from Simon's Rock College of Bard.

"The brochure was very inviting," he says. So he and his mother visited the campus. "Everyone at Simon's Rock was just so friendly," Rodney says. It was very different from what he'd been experiencing in New York. "It was actually exciting to just say 'hello' to people you didn't know. It made me very happy, and as I was being interviewed, I felt as if I were being treated as if I were older. I realized I was applying to a normal college."

Rodney received the DuBois Scholarship and became a freshman (or "freshling," as first year students are called) at 16.

His Brooklyn friends and teachers were surprised by Rodney's decision to go to Simon's Rock. Even though none of them knew anything about the college, they told Rodney he was making a big mistake. They thought that getting a liberal arts education instead of a scientific one was not a wise thing to do. "But not for me," says Rodney. "I felt there were so many things I wanted to learn that weren't available at my high school. I felt stifled." His mother was completely won over the day of their visit. "She knew I'd like it here."

■ Following in His Sister's Footsteps

Tim Ryan, about whom you read in Chapter VII, was identified as "gifted and talented" in math while he was in elementary school. By the time he'd entered his Groton, New York, junior high school, he was taking algebra. Then he started accelerating in other subjects as well. By the time he was 16, he'd completed virtually all of his required high school subjects and had taken his SATs.

Tim's older sister had also been a gifted and talented student. She'd been accepted into the University of Delaware as an early admissions student several years before. So Tim says, "I'm going to do that too. There was always competition between us. I couldn't stand to have my sister do something I couldn't do."

With Tim's terrific test scores and his ability to talk his way into sounding like a serious student, he was a shoo-in at the University of Delaware.

■ Getting Away from a Place You Don't Like

Kim Cooper, who completed two of the "happiest years of my life" at the TAMS and started as a junior in biology at Cornell University in the fall of 1996, came from the tiny town (population 3,500) of West (which is actually north of Waco, Texas). "It is the kolacky capital of the world," says Kim. (Kolacky, Kim explains, is a Czech specialty—a fried dough that is stuffed with meat and other things.) "My old high school had about 100 kids in the class. Our science labs were pathetic. They hadn't been updated since the 1950s. West is a town where sports is king, and the folks there keep voting to build new sports facilities. There was nothing there for me."

One of the most exciting aspects of TAMS was that "for the first time I met really intelligent students, and we didn't get the grief we had experienced in our regular high schools. Here you can be yourself. No one will pick on you because you are bright. One night a bunch of us stayed up talking about what it was like for us in our home high school—and we all found that we'd had difficulties. Most people didn't understand us. So it was important to find out that we'd all gone through some rough times. You know, most of us came here because we wanted to get away from a place we didn't like. Now that I've graduated, I can tell you that we'd do this again because of all the friends we've made."

■ All His Friends Had Left

Andy Pasqual of Clarkson, Georgia, was already dissatisfied with his high school when he received a letter from the Advanced Academy of Georgia. "We (he and his parents) had already been looking for alternatives because my school wasn't working out. I wasn't being challenged, and a lot of my friends had left. Several had moved to the next county over." When he read the letter describing the Academy, he thought, "Wow! This looks pretty cool. It said that the Academy was for advanced high school students and that you could live there and take courses for college credit." His visit to the campus confirmed his belief that this place was for him. In fact, some of his teachers from his high school encouraged him to move on. Also, his voice teacher at his high school was leaving, and that was another reason for Andy's desire to leave, too.

"I was going to sacrifice my last two years of high school and I wouldn't be able to do some of my favorite high school activities."

"I knew there would be a trade-off," Andy says. "I was going to sacrifice my last two years of high school and I wouldn't be able to do some of my favorite high school activities any more." One thing that especially bothered him was the National Honor Society. "I was pretty much in the running to be the next year's president, and when my sponsor found I was applying to this program, they wouldn't even let me run. I was being separated out. I didn't feel too good about that."

There were some other trade-offs as well. For one thing, there were curfews at the Academy—11 p.m. on weekdays; 12 p.m. weekends. And you are not allowed to do varsity sports, nor can you join a sorority or fraternity—except for a service fraternity. Anyone found drinking alcohol or using drugs is automatically dismissed from the program. These restrictions didn't bother Andy. In fact, to him "the Academy seemed like this extra-long summer camp, only you had to study.

"I had a great time at West Georgia. I was so challenged. It was," he admits, "a lot harder than I thought. I got involved in a lot of things. I joined the Chamber Singers (the college chorus). And it was the first time they had had high school kids in their chorus."

Andy also liked the fact that the regular college students and the professors didn't know who the Academy students were unless the student told someone. "People assumed I was a college student." And when people did find out, "most thought it was pretty cool. But other students had a different experience.

> "I had a great time at West Georgia. I was so challenged. I got involved in a lot of things."

Some professors did resent the fact that high school kids were in their classes."

Andy learned that it was important to keep in touch with his home school. "Otherwise you can lose out on scholarship and other financial aid that may be available to you as a high school student." He also thought it might be a good idea for early college students to "have in mind the college they want to go to when they finish the early college part. This is because some four-year colleges won't accept early college credits from the Academy." If that happens, you will have to begin your four-year college as a freshman.

Andy chose Furman University in South Carolina when he completed the two years at the Academy. Furman accepted virtually all 62 credits, allowing him to enter with junior standing. However, Andy intends to stay at Furman for four years because he is doing a double major in music and chemistry. While he expects to follow a career in medicine, "music is something that I love. If I ever do anything with my music, it will be as a music minister." Despite the fact that he has junior rank, "I feel as if I'm more at home with the freshman class."

CHOOSING A STUDY ABROAD PROGRAM INSTEAD OF EARLY COLLEGE

Laura Weeldreyer was an excellent student at her high school in rural Hickory, North Carolina. The trouble was, she didn't have to put much effort into her studies. "There just weren't very high standards," she says. "Most of the students did not plan on going on to college because Hickory is a big mill town and a center of furniture production for North Carolina. So people who don't go to college can make an excellent living there." Laura says that there was a lot of emphasis on sports, and "I wasn't into being a cheerleader. So I was pretty unhappy, and didn't find a lot of satisfaction in school. I was looking for a way out as soon as possible."

Since she had already completed all of the requirements for high school graduation in her junior year, Laura decided to check out getting into college early. "I did this all on my own. There wasn't any guidance counselor to help me." Since she had visited some relatives in Boston, she decided to apply to Boston University, and was accepted there. "But I hadn't thought through how it would be with the low expectations of my high school to go to a high-powered college. And I hadn't thought about financial aid, and how expensive it would be to be so far from home."

When Laura told her mother that she'd been accepted to BU, her mom asked, "Have you really thought about this?" So they sat down and talked about what other options Laura might have. "She didn't say no, you can't go, because that probably wouldn't have been very effective. Instead my mother said, 'have you thought about how it is going to be—16 going to a college in a rigorous academic environment?'" Instead, her mother offered her the option of becoming an exchange student in a foreign country. This had actually been a choice Laura's mom had turned down when she was a high school student because she had been too shy.

Through a coworker at a bookstore where Laura had a part-time job, she found out about a program called Experiment in International Living based in Brattleboro, Vermont (Currently, this program offers only summer programs abroad to high school students). The sticking point was that Laura had to meet their language requirement. Although Laura had taken French in high school, it wasn't enough to be in the program in France. So she used a small inheritance from her grandfather to take all the French classes offered at the local college during the rest of her junior year and during the summer—and that fall she met the ten other students at Kennedy airport and was off to Paris. "It was very scary," Laura recalls. "Everybody's parents left." Laura and her mom had packed her carry-on bag the night before. "They (the program) had strict requirements about how much stuff you could bring, and I had really stretched it to the nth degree. My mom and I had packed this bag as if we were doing surgery or something, and the bag was so dense, the people who inspect the luggage couldn't see through it. So they made me unpack it—even the presents I'd brought for my host family.

"I was sitting on the floor of Kennedy Airport with all my belongings and no idea how I'm going to get them back in this bag because my mother had already left. So I had to try really hard not to have a breakdown. I did, eventually, get everything repacked."

Finally, though, the ten students plus one adult advisor, were airborne. "They had had a bunch of bombings (in Paris) and we were advised to 'try not to look American'. So we all started smoking immediately!" Laura discovered that she was one of the youngest kids in the program, and that her French was the worst. "I was freaked out by that." But "the one thing I have is pride, and to go home and go back to school after I'd made this huge deal about being the first exchange student from my high school—if nothing else, pride will do a lot to keep a person from giving up."

After a three-week session at a language institute in the city of Tours, Laura and one other student were placed with families in Colmar, close to the German border. Laura didn't always enjoy her living situation because the host family didn't make their rules clear at the outset. For example, her family only used the telephone for quick messages, not for long chats with friends. And, unlike phone companies in most cities in the U.S. which don't charge for local calls, all phone calls in France are charged by the minute. Of course, once she understood the problem, Laura used a phone card and called her friends from a pay phone, but the damage to their relationship was already done. In hindsight, Laura says it would have been better if she had been more proactive by asking questions first.

However, going to the local high school turned out to be exciting in several different ways. French students are very serious about their studies, and Laura "learned what it meant to be a serious student. The senior year in a French high school is very intense. It's like going to college."

There were two important things that happened while she was there. The first of these was a "huge student strike. It was the biggest student strike since 1968—and it was over the fact that the minister of education wanted to charge tuition in the colleges, which had always been free." The strike soon spread to Belgium and Germany. It was really amazing. The students actually closed the schools for three weeks and we marched around the town and sat in the middle of intersections— that's when I really bonded with the other students. The strike was totally organized by the high school students. They were saying, 'we won't accept that. And we have power.'

"And the second thing that happened was just before I left they threw this huge celebration party in my honor. People brought me presents. People wrote cards and they did things which totally made me cry. They remembered when I first came, and we talked about stereotypes—the ones I held about the French and those they held about Americans (reruns of Dallas were big, and they all wanted to know if I had an oil well in my backyard). They remembered that I said I thought that there would be French men waiting for me at the airport who would drink champagne from my shoe, write me beautiful poems, and send me flowers. Well, two boys in the class wrote me poems and they read them to the entire class. It was so funny and sweet."

While Laura was in France, she kept in close touch with her mother who kept track of when applications to colleges were due. She was accepted at several colleges, and decided on New York University. Laura was now confident that she could handle the challenge of both New York City and a tough university program.

■ **The Experiment in International Living**
World Learning
Kipling Road
PO Box 676
Brattleboro, VT 05302-0676
Phone: 800/345-2929
Fax: 802/258-3428
E-mail: eil@worldlearning.org
Web site: http://www.worldlearning.org/ip/summer.html
Note: EIL now only offers summer abroad programs in 25 differ-
ent countries for high school students.

EARLY COLLEGE IS NOT A PICNIC

Just because you have left a place you didn't like and are now a college student, doesn't mean your problems are over. Many students worried they'd flunk out. Others were concerned about making friends. And almost all were shocked at how much time it took to study.

Rodney was afraid, "I was no longer going to do as well as I'd been doing, and that everyone was going to be smarter than me. And I was afraid people wouldn't be interested in the things I was." He was also afraid that "people were going to realize that I was poor and that would matter."

Most of his fears were unfounded. Twenty-one percent of the students at Simon's Rock entering his freshman class were minority students. "Sometimes I feel I'm in a sea of white faces, and other times it doesn't matter. Sometimes I have to adapt to what they want to do, although it is difficult to get [white kids] to adapt to what I want to do."

Just as Rodney found some of the white students had notions about African Americans, he also learned to confront his own stereotypes since he's been at Simon's Rock. "I didn't know that everyone has something worthwhile to say. I thought only those people with money, only those people who had some position of power were worth listening to. I know better now." And "even though we each come to college from vastly different backgrounds, the shared experience of college is an important basis for friendship."

Many of Leela's problems stemmed from her "quirky" alternative school education. "I almost flunked out during my first semester at Ithaca College. I didn't have the standard background, and I couldn't always understand what the professor wanted. In one class I had a D- at midterm. But by the end of the semester I had a B because the professor talked to me. I'd completely misunderstood how to write a paper." But by her sophomore year, she'd gotten so skilled at writing papers that she was offered a job in the writing lab helping less able students. By her junior year she declared a major in philosophy. "I wanted to learn logical thinking. I felt the discipline that could help me most was one that would teach me to think and reason and write logical papers. Thinking and reasoning—with those two skills I could go on to anything." Not surprisingly, the career Leela chose was law. Today she is an assistant attorney general for the state of Texas.

Kim Cooper admits her first year was tough. "It took me an entire year

"You will have to study seven hours for exams, and do at least two hours a night of homework for each course."

to learn how to study. You will have to study seven hours for exams, and do at least two hours a night of homework for each course. But the great thing is that at TAMS you have a lot of people to study with. Yet, all of the togetherness can also present problems. If you have an argument with someone, you will have to see that person every day. Living together forces you to work things out. And dating couples have problems when they break up. The thing is, you can't hide from your problems here. You have to find people to help you."

Kathleen Harpenau, who is in her second year at the TALH program at Lamar University, says that some students who come to TALH aren't responsible. "They don't go to classes, and when they find out that there is no one here to bail them out, and no mother to tell you to get up and go to class, they will fail. In this place, the more you put into it, the more you'll get out. "

Sometimes students who attend the early college programs feel hemmed in when restrictions are placed on their social lives. TAMS, TALH, PEG at Mary Baldwin, The Clarkson School, and the Advanced Academy of Georgia, for example, have curfews and special programs just for the younger students. While many students feel the rules are quite liberal—more liberal than they have at home—others feel there shouldn't be restrictions on their time.

Shawn and his brother, Scott Mattot, both were accepted at The Clarkson School in different years. Neither liked the family atmosphere that is consciously fostered there. Scott says, "They do crazy things at Clarkson. They want all the students to feel like a family. Now the dorms are great. We lived in four-person suites. However, we were discouraged from meeting the regular freshmen. But the freshmen are really nice. Shawn also felt uncomfortable with the "family" atmosphere. "I didn't care for the family atmosphere. I didn't adjust to that very well. They try to get you all to be friends. But my cousin was going to Clarkson, so I hung out with him and his friends."

Other students love the family atmosphere at their colleges. Kathleen Harpenau says, "At TALH there are 100 other students here like me. We have family groups and we discuss our problems and bond with each other. Basically we get to know a bigger family of 100 people."

Tim Ryan used his time at the University of Delaware to make lots of friends. Since he didn't find the academics especially difficult, he found himself cutting classes and goofing off. "The trouble was, I just wasn't motivated to do college work," he says. "I was looking to have fun and get out from under my parents' supervision." Tim dropped out of college after a year and worked for some time before he joined the Air Force.

COLLEGE COURSES ARE REAL WORK—THEY MAKE YOU THINK

Virtually all of the students reported that their college courses were harder than anything else they'd undertaken. At the same time, they said the challenge was exhilarating. Moreover, the students expressed relief to be out of a place where they didn't want to be and in an atmosphere where they were valued for their intellectual abilities.

"My experience here has been wonderful. For two years I've been living with all my best friends," says Kim.

"In my experience, it is the best thing that ever happened in my life," says Kathleen.

"You really did have to work, and you really did have to think," says Lorin, who received her bachelor's degree at the University of Chicago by the time she was 20 and also earned a mas-

"In my experience, it is the best thing that ever happened in my life."

ter's degree. At 25, Lorin is a vice-president in charge of corporate invest-
ments for a large bank in Cleveland, Ohio.

Some Tips for Parents

- *Don't worry about the "pedigree" of the college. Worry about whether your kids are intellectually alive.*

- *Remember that most highly motivated kids are really finished with the normal high school curriculum halfway through eleventh grade.*

- *Visit with your child at the college he or she is interested in attending.*

- *Talk to other parents whose children have gone to college before completing high school. Get a variety of opinions from parents, guidance counselors, college administrators, and students—especially students.*

- *Most of all, be sensitive to the needs of your own son or daughter.*

Chapter IX

Taking The Plunge: I'm Ready For College

WHAT DO I DO NOW?

THERE ARE SMART AND DUMB WAYS TO CHOOSE A COLLEGE. "The first time I applied to college," says Jeff Finlay of Raleigh, North Carolina, "I figured that one place was as good as another. So I applied to three state universities because the applications were easy to fill out. I was accepted at only one of them, so that didn't give me much of a choice. Still, I went off with the unrealistic expectation that by just being in college, I'd become an educated person. I got an education, all right, but not the kind I was interested in. What I learned from that experience was that I had to value myself, and I had to value learning. When I transferred the following year, I chose my college with great care."

As Jeff found out, you will probably get accepted to at least one college any way you approach the problem. (There are, after all, about 3,500 colleges in the U.S.) Michael Urgo made that discovery, too, when he accepted an offer from Hampton City College in Virginia just because he didn't know what else to do. However, you owe it to yourself (that's right! yourself—not your parents, your teachers, or your friends) to make an informed and thoughtful decision. After all, you and/or your parents will be paying hard-earned dollars for your college education. If you take out student loans to help finance college, you want to feel confident that the education you receive is worth your time and the expense. Those college loans take years to pay off after you graduate. In today's college market, taking out student loans is a simple fact of life.

A student loan may be the very best investment you will ever make. According to Edward B. Fiske, author of *Best Buys in College Education*, "Just about any college can be considered a bargain. . . . Figures from the Bureau of the Census show that the typical college graduate can expect to earn nearly 40 percent more than a high school graduate over the course of a lifetime." And, incidentally, a college education will make you a more interesting person.

If you attend a state university, you can expect, along with your diploma, at least $10,000 worth of debt. You must begin to pay that back within six months after graduation (unless you go on to graduate school, in which case you won't start paying on your loans until you complete your degree). That $10,000 actually translates into $14,000 plus, if it is a guaranteed student loan from a bank at the current 8 percent interest rate.

NOT THE COLLEGE OF YOUR DREAMS?

Even if you think you've made a wise choice, your college may not live up to your expectations once you get there. This is not the end of the world. You can stay at the less-than-perfect-college for a year, then transfer. In fact, if you get excellent grades, you may be able to get into a more demanding school.

That's what happened to Kiran Sigmon from Raleigh, North Carolina. She'd spent a year between high school and college working and traveling all over New Zealand, where she was part of an organization called Operation Raleigh (now defunct), and then went on to China, where she earned room and board and a little spending money by teaching English to college students at the university in Hun Zjo, before finally linking up with a group called Students of the World. When she finally returned home, Kiran didn't want to attend any of the colleges in her home state. She was still on an adventure kick. So she applied to colleges in places that sounded exotic. "I boiled it down to three: the University of Colorado, the University of Hawaii, and the University of Maine. I was only looking at colleges for where they were located. I figured that if I were going to other places in the world, I kind of wanted to see what it was like in our country. I'd lived in the South all of my life, and Maine seemed like a place far away from everything. So I chose Maine."

Kiran arrived on campus full of hope and eager to make new friends. "Because of the New Zealand and China experience, where we were thrown into situations and had to rely on each other, I was able to form strong friendships quickly. I was kind of expecting the same thing when I came to Maine," she says. "I found that not everyone was anxious to make new friends and work together. So it was really hard." Kiran also discovered that there were many required courses before she'd be able to take the ones she wanted.

Even before the first semester was over, Kiran applied to a small college not too far from her hometown, one where she was able to plan out her own major. Despite her disappointment with her first college choice, Kiran says, "I turned that frustration into an understanding that I was asking too much of too big a place. I learned a lot about Maine, and I've learned a lot on my own. I'm able to think more clearly about my needs and my life's direction." Kiran has since decided on a career in medicine and is pursuing that profession.

If you and your college are a mismatch, don't throw in the towel after a couple of uninspired weeks. What you need to do is figure out why you and your college aren't in sync. Did you have unrealistic expectations? Is it the institution itself? Are the students not interested in the same kinds of things you are? Have you reconsidered your major interests? Once you get a handle on the problem, you can take steps

Transferring Is One Way to Graduate from a More Demanding College

■ *A student with a lackluster academic record or average SAT scores may improve his or her chances of getting into a more prestigious college or university by attending a community college or less difficult college for a year or two. According to Helene Reynolds, an education consultant in Princeton, New Jersey, "This is an excellent way to improve your chances. If you are able to achieve a 3.0 or 3.5 average, then you can present yourself to a better college. By then, no one is going to look at your SATs or high school work," she says. "And you have an opportunity to create a new record."*

■ *Colleges often look for transfer students with specific kinds of skills or majors. Says Ms. Reynolds, "Transfer admissions fill a different need within a school." A college may be looking for a tuba player, or the captain of the chess team, or somebody to major in French."*

■ *Many colleges have lower admission standards if you are willing to enter in January (for those on the semester system) or in March (for those on the quarter system). This is because colleges always lose freshmen students during the first semester.*

to correct it. Do keep one important thing in mind: you can't change the way things are done at a college all by yourself, and you can't change the mindset of the other students. The only thing you can change is yourself—that involves a change of attitude.

On the other hand, perhaps you have taken stock of yourself, your grades, or your finances and decided to attend a less expensive/commuting college before heading off to the one from which you intend to graduate. This can be a very wise decision. While the first college you attend may not be your dream place, you at least are grounded in why you are there, even though you are pretty certain that you will transfer after a year or two.

THINK IT THROUGH

The best way to think about choosing a college is to look at who you are and what kind of an atmosphere you'd like to be in. Don't get drawn in by the latest fad in colleges. No kidding! Colleges are subject to fads among certain groups of juniors and seniors. For several years Brown University will be hot. Another year it will be Reed College. Of course, both of these are excellent schools—but there are literally thousands of fine colleges that are not on the "hot button" list but may be just the place for you. Since you are probably a pretty independent person, you should be more interested in finding the school that suits your needs than in impressing the neighbors with a "brand name" college. Sure, a degree from one of the Ivies will impress a lot of people, including your first future employer, more than a diploma from What's-it U, but how well you do in the adult working world still depends on how well you use your own innate gifts. Don't be afraid to look into some off-the-beaten-track colleges.

If you are a person who stopped out for a while, you've already figured out that your education is really in your own hands. Your mind isn't a sausage casing into which some wise old professor will stuff her or his lifelong learning. You, yourself, will bring to your college experience the desire to learn, and much of what you accomplish will be because you've thought about your unique qualities during the break from schools.

Those of you choosing the early college option must pick your college with great care. Even more than the "Johnnie-come-lately" types, you need to pay close attention to the social aspects of the college you choose. Consultant Helene Reynolds cautions that the "social environment into which you are going has to be just right. It can't be a college that is going to just promote the intellect. It also should enhance the student's growth." Whether an early college goer, a late one, or right on the mark, you want to make the most informed choice you can.

Larry Colman of Winnetka, Illinois, was an early admission student at the University of Chicago, which has a long history of encouraging younger students. He had, like Lorin Dytel, just turned 16, and was tremendously excited about going there. "I'd gone for a campus visit," he says, "during one of those weekends the university sets up for prospective students. It was such a great experience. I met dozens of kids who shared my interests, and I spent hours involved in amazing discussions. I was absolutely convinced that this was the place for me."

"I met dozens of kids who shared my interests."

By the end of the first semester, Larry had serious doubts about continuing at Chicago. "I could deal with the workload, even though it was sometimes staggering. What was so hard for me was that I had so little social life. Freshmen women weren't interested in dating freshmen guys—especially guys who are younger than they are. [And remember what Lorin said—many more guys than gals.] And I just didn't know where to meet girls my own age."

Larry decided to take time out after he completed his first year—and actually found that despite his unhappiness with the social scene, "I really did quite a bit of growing up." A year later, he was ready to go back. "After all," he says, "now I'm an upperclassman. And freshmen women don't think of me as a kid."

College Tuition: More or Less

According to The American Council on Education, many people think college costs are higher than they actually are.

Here are some nationwide average annual tuition costs for the 1998-99 academic year:

■ *Two-year public colleges: $1,633*

■ *Four-year public universities: $3,243*

■ *Four-year private universities: $14,508*

These fees are for tuition only.

SOME QUESTIONS TO THINK ABOUT

1. Am I ready for college now? (If your answer is "no," decide just how firm that "no" is. Some people aren't ready for college until they set foot on campus.)

2. Do I want to live at home and attend college, or is living on a college campus a priority?

3. Do I want a liberal arts education, or do I have a specific career in mind for which a specific college major can prepare me? Is that specific training all that I want from my education? Many educators

and business executives prefer students with a liberal arts education. Specific jobs skills can be learned at the workplace. Many professions require graduate school.

4. What is my financial situation? Can I (and my family) cope with the high tuition of a private college or university? Don't be put off by what you hear about high tuition in private colleges. For one thing, there are many scholarships available, as well as work-study options. There are also many fine private colleges and universities with moderate tuition. Two books by Edward Fiske can point you in the right direction: *The Best Buys in College Education* and *The Selective Guide to Colleges*.

5. Do I want to stay in my home state or explore another part of the country? If you opt for the latter, be sure to figure in the cost of home visits when making out your budget. Be aware that the highest airfare and the most difficult time to book flights occur at Thanksgiving, Christmas, and Easter.

6. Will I be eligible for scholarships and financial aid?

7. Am I looking for a college that will allow me a considerable amount of choice in selecting my courses, or do I want a college where there are stiff requirements so I'll be forced to study certain subjects I might not take on my own?

8. Is there a specific college I really want to attend?

9. Is there a specific college my parents want me to attend? Is that a place I'd like to go?

10. Do my SAT (or ACT) scores really reflect my academic abilities?

11. What are my special skills and talents that would be worth noting on a college application to make me stand out from other applicants in my range?

12. Do I want to aim for a college that is very competitive academically or one without the pressure of having to elbow my way into an A?

13. Do I want a very large, impersonal university where I can melt into the background, a small intimate one where everybody knows everybody else, or one in between?

14. Do I want a college where people come from all parts of the country or a region different from mine? Believe it or not, regional differences can be tricky, especially when it comes to food. Sprouts on a Kosher corned beef sandwich on rye in Santa Cruz seemed mighty strange to someone used to the delis in New York City or Teaneck, New Jersey. Another Yankee, who chose to go south to college, complained about grits and gravy being served every morning at breakfast.

15. Am I going to be happy in a college where fraternities and sororities are a major part of the social scene? Or, conversely, in a setting where they are not?

16. Do I want a college that offers a chance to get involved with the local community?

17. Do I need to be sure there are people who belong to the same religious faith and ethnic group as I do? Or will it be enough to know that outside the college community, I can find my own religious or ethnic group?

18. Will I want to look for organizations on campus that reflect my political ideals?

19. If I go to college far from home, will I mind not seeing my family more than once or twice a year? If the dorms close down over Christmas and Easter, will I have a place to stay?

20. Do I want to test the waters in a community college first before attending a high-powered four-year college?

After you've answered these questions, go back to your self-assessment test and take it again. How do the answers to these questions mesh with your profile on the assessment sheets? If you think you have a pretty good idea of what you are looking for in a college, you are ready for the next step.

INFORMATION GATHERING

There are all kinds of ways to research the college market. Even if you have been out of school for a couple of years, you may go back to your high school guidance counselor and seek her or his advice. Many schools have sophisticated software programs that can help you narrow your selection as you type in your interests, financial requirements, and other pertinent information. And you can always do your own research right on the Web, although that can be a somewhat tedious process, with more choices than you are really comfortable with.

There are numerous books and magazines that can provide you with information, including *Making a Difference College Guide,* by Miriam Weinstein, a book of selected colleges that offer courses designed to help you make the world a better place. Of course there is *Barron's Profiles of American Colleges,* which describes more than 1,500 colleges, and the many Peterson's Guides, as well. Sometimes, however, these books can be overwhelming. There are other ways to explore your options, including talking to friends and relatives about their college experiences. As well, when you find a college that interests you, you can do a thorough exploration of it on the Web, and even e-mail students there to get the lowdown from a student point-of-view.

Ten Tips For Exploring Colleges on the Net

Douglas Fireside, who teachers computer skills to students, offers these suggestions.

1. Use a good search engine. A lot of the work has already been done by others. Why replicate it? Use Yahoo (http://www.yahoo.com),

Snap (http://www.snap.com), or one of the other larger search engines to help sort things out. Follow the links they already have for finding a specific college or for other information.

2. It pays to know what you are looking for. Are you looking for information on financial aid? Do you already know an area of the country (or other countries) you are interested in researching? Are you looking for a big school or a smaller college? The Web is vast and you can spend (or waste) a lot of time looking around. One good way to do this is to search with as many "keywords" as you can to narrow down your results. Don't just search for "colleges." Try "Colleges Maryland," for example.

3. There is a lot of FREE information about financial aid. For example try: http://www.ed.gov/prog_info/SFA/StudentGuide/1998-9/index.html. This links you to *The Student Guide,* an on line publication put out by the federal government. It is designed to outline the programs that the Feds have created to help you (and/or your parents) pay for college. (If you don't have Internet access, you can call the following toll-free number to obtain a hard copy of The Student Guide: 800/4-FED-AID. Another source I found with a lot of info: http://www.finaid.org/

There are plenty of other places for information. A quick search turned up over 400 sites. Again, read carefully. If you can, narrow down your search (see tip #2).

IMPORTANT: Do not pay (or give your credit card number) for information about financial aid. You can get this same information for free from other sources.

4. Use a college or university Web site for all it is worth! If you are interested in a college and would like to find out about campus life, some sites allow you to e-mail resident life directors, see which professors are teaching in a program you are interested in, as well as other things.

5. Use the Web when you need to find specialized information. If you are looking for a traditional Black college try: http://www.edonline.com/cq/hbcu/

This site connects you with historically Black colleges and universities. It also has information on finding financial aid.

Looking for women's colleges? Try using Yahoo. A quick search turned up an impressive list of sites.

6. Not sure where to start? Try this site: http//www.globalcomputing.com/universy.html. This site allows you to check a lot of the college Web sites by clicking on a region of the country. A great way to cut through the clutter. Simply click on a state and a list comes up!

7. Some schools have multiple sites. Some have e-mail links that allow you to find e-mail to students and professors. Some list entrance requirements, financial aid information, etc. CAUTION: Don't judge a school solely by its Web site. Call, talk to alums or students who are there now. BEST yet, visit the school.

8. If a school doesn't have the information on its sites (and a few might not—gulp—even have a site at all!) don't give up. Get a nice new notebook to use for your Web searches. Take notes. Remember to write down phone numbers and addresses of schools that look interesting to you. Schools are happy to send you information by snail mail.

9. Remember that Web addresses change faster than Web search engines can keep up. Most school sites stay around but the content changes. It pays to check back if you visited a site more than a month ago. Links to "campus life" areas might change frequently—some of these link up to businesses near the school.

10. Read the FAQ for a school or other education site. This is a common tool used on the Web to list the basics about a site. Most people don't bother, and yet, most should.

Gerard Turbide, senior assistant director of admissions at Ithaca College (New York), says that the big plus for seeking out information about a college on line is the interactive flavor. "A big plus is that you can have contact with faculty and students." He also notes the advantage a prospective student has of being able to get information in a very flexible manner, i.e., he or she can get the information about a college at any time—10:00 p.m. or midnight, if that works. Turbide also stresses that all e-mail sent to the admissions office is read and answered personally by admissions counselors. But he also stresses that nothing replaces a campus visit, although the virtual college tour is a nice complement to the real thing.

SHOULD I SEEK OUT A COLLEGE CONSULTANT?

You may also want to find a professional educational consultant, who for a fee is trained to help you find the right college. Guided by your interests, SAT or ACT scores, and your personality, a consultant can take a lot of the guesswork out of the process. A good consultant focuses on your individual needs, has lots of experience in helping students find a suitable college, has visited at least 100 colleges and universities around the country, and is up-to-date on at least as many others. Of course, anybody can hang out a shield and call themselves a "college consultant"—so you have to shop carefully. You want a consultant who is not only skilled in helping you find the right school but who also continually updates his or her knowledge of the college scene.

"Of course, anybody can hang out a shield and call themselves a college consultant."

One organization that will provide you with a list of professional educational consultants is the Independent Educational Consultants Association (IECA). You can contact the Association at 4085 Chain Bridge Road, Suite 401, Fairfax, VA 22030, Phone: 703/591-4850, Fax: 703/591-4860, E-mail: iecaassoc@aol.com, Web site: http://www.educationalconsulting.org/.

Although most people do just fine on their own, or with help from their high school guidance counselors or friends, there are situations when a college consultant can be of enormous help.

Mark Sklarow, executive director of IECA, says, "Nobody really knows everything about the thousands of college and post-high school programs that are out there. A good educational consultant is an expert matchmaker. He or she can help you figure out your particular needs." Members of IECA are constantly updating their information by visiting campuses, taking workshops, and sharing information with other members. Many consultants specialize in certain areas, such as placing students with disabilities or special needs.

If you and your parents seem to be at odds over the colleges you are choosing, or if you are looking for an interesting program before you go off to college, a consultant can help you and your family sort out things. If you really aren't at all sure where you would fit in, a college consultant can help.

Special Situations

Perhaps the best reason to choose a consultant is if you are a person with special needs, such as being gifted and talented, have had a non-traditional education, such as attending alternative schools, have been home-schooled, or are challenged by a specific learning or physical disability. Because people with disabilities are now guaranteed their civil rights by federal law, every college that receives federal funds must provide some special support services and accommodations for students with disabilities. Thus, while many colleges will tell you they have special programs, it can take an expert to evaluate them. A savvy consultant can save you endless months of frustration.

The following is a clearinghouse on postsecondary education for individuals with disabilities and is funded by the U.S. Department of Education.

- **Heath Resource Center**
  American Council on Education
  One Dupont Circle, Suite 800
  Washington, DC 20036-1193
  Phone: 202/939-9320 and 800/544-3284
  Voice TT available
  Web site: http://www.acenet.edu/

IF YOU HAVE BEEN HOME-SCHOOLED

If you are one of the many students who have been "uniquely" educated either at home or in a non-traditional school setting, you will find that much of the college application form simply doesn't apply to you. And you will have to find a way to prove to the admissions people that you are ready and qualified to pursue a college degree. This is where you will want to get as much information as possible from the admissions officers before you file your application. Without traditional grades to show to a prospective college, or without your teacher recommendations to add, you will have to rely on two things: your personal essay and your SAT or ACT scores. You might also want to find out if the colleges you are applying to will be willing to look at a portfolio of your work. "Home-schooled students present all sorts of interesting problems," says Mark Sklarow, and in his discussions with admissions officers finds that they "are trying to figure out how to fit them in." He finds that colleges are accepting small numbers of home-school students—but it is up to the student to show that he or she has acquired the skills needed to succeed.

CHECK OUT COLLEGE CATALOGS

Once you have an idea of several colleges you'd like to apply to, you can spend some time reading through a variety of college catalogs, or read the college catalog on the Internet. Both methods have their advantages and disadvantages. You can request a paper catalog directly from specific colleges or check them in your public library or school guidance office. Make sure you get current catalogs. (After your SAT or ACT scores are in, your mail box will be filled with them.) Most colleges and universities have Web sites and post their catalogs on them, plus some very interesting stuff that can't be found in the paper version. Both versions tell you a great deal if you know what you are looking for.

You can see what the campus looks like, the kinds of students it attracts (all have smiling students), the academic priorities, fees, living arrangements, outside activities, courses offered, and much more.

Rodney Christopher remarks that the catalog from Simon's Rock was very "inviting." He had never heard of the college before, but after reading through it, he was eager for the next step: a campus visit. That catalog was crucial to getting him onto the campus.

When Doug Leonard decided to head south to study in North Carolina, he sent for several catalogs and narrowed his choice to two possibilities. "I did this on the basis of the city where I wanted to be, the size of the school I thought would be best for me, and the kinds of courses they had to offer. Of course, the fact that the University of North Carolina in Greensboro had a ratio of three women for every man was definitely part of the equation," he notes with a happy grin. "And that last bit of information was in the catalog."

How to Read a College Catalog

College catalogs are meant to entice you. They are filled with photos of beautiful buildings, laughing students, and winning athletic teams. They are advertisements for the college. But they offer a great deal of solid information. For example, you can find out:

1. **How many professors have Ph.Ds. How many are full-time members of the faculty and how many are part-time "adjunct professors."**

2. **From which colleges the professors graduated.**

3. **The student-faculty ratio.**

4. **If the department you are interested in has enough professors who reflect different viewpoints. (This can be learned from the kinds of courses offered, as well as the universities which trained the professors.)**

5. **If there is a core curriculum.**

6. **If there is an overall philosophy in the college.**

7. **If there is a multicultural approach to learning and to the student body.**

8. **If there is a study abroad program.**

9. **If there is an honor society.**

10. **If there are extracurricular activities that appeal to you.**

11. **If there are requirements you feel are not what you need or want.**

12. **If transfer credit from summer college courses or study abroad is obtainable.**

13. **If there is a senior honor's project.**

14. **If off-campus internships are available.**

15. If there are adequate library resources, or if there is access to other nearby college libraries.

16. If there is a physical education requirement.

17. If writing skills are emphasized.

18. If the size and location of the school is right for you.

19. If the religious, racial, or ethnic group you belong to is represented on campus.

20. If the pricetag is within your target range.

21. If there is adequate financial aid available.

Even if you are savvy enough to dig out all of the good information in the catalog, it alone will not tell you everything. Check out some of the college guide books. They will tell you how competitive the colleges are. *Profiles of American Colleges* ranks colleges by "most competitive, highly competitive, very competitive and competitive, less competitive, noncompetitive, and special." (This last category is made up of professional schools of music and art.)

"Don't be afraid to talk to professors. You are the reason they have a job."

ARE CAMPUS VISITS IMPORTANT?

If there are two or three colleges in one area that seem interesting, arrange your campus visits during the same week. Phone or write the admissions office. Request a campus tour, an interview with an admissions officer, permission to sit in on classes, and the opportunity to talk to professors who teach subjects that interest you. Don't be afraid to talk to professors. You are the reason they have a job. They love to talk about what they teach—especially to an interested prospective student. And if you happen to have read something a professor has written, and you feel comfortable mentioning it, you will have made his or her day!

Be sure to talk to other students. You may be able to stay on campus overnight. Oh, yes, when you show up for an interview, dress casually—but keep your shirt tails tucked in. If you have specific needs or special concerns, write them down, so you won't forget to ask about them.

Checking out several colleges during a single week proved extremely helpful to Doug. Among his North Carolina possibilities was one in Raleigh. He had already been accepted there before he visited the campus. "I was really disappointed once I saw the place," Doug says. "Even though I'd written ahead and phoned to make sure the admissions people knew I was coming, when I got there they seemed totally disinterested in me. They did nothing to make me want to go there. On the other hand, from the moment I set foot on the UNC campus at Greensboro, I felt at home. Everybody from the admissions people to the students and the professors I talked to seemed to want me to come here. One of the professors in my field of communications had read my application. She even remembered that I'd had some experience as a DJ back home. 'I can't wait until you come here,' she said. She really made me feel as if my time away from school was well spent.

"It was such a welcoming atmosphere. I knew this was the place for me. Even though it was a fairly small campus, Greensboro is a real city, and there seemed to be a lot of stuff going on there."

> "It was such a welcoming atmosphere. I knew this was the place for me."

Doug's perception of the university and the city proved correct for his objectives. Over the years he made strong friendships, took classes that were both enjoyable and challenging—and found time to start a weekly newspaper with a group of like-minded students. One summer he remained in Greensboro to work at a local radio station and study. He got a kick out of conducting campus tours for prospective students. "As a Yankee, I wanted to be able to return the kind of hospitality I'd received." After Doug graduated from UNC-G, he spent a year splitting his time between working at a television station in Raleigh and the radio station where he'd interned.

HOW MANY COLLEGES SHOULD I APPLY TO?

Until a few years ago, most college-bound students felt safe applying to three or four colleges. One of these was always called the "safety" school—often the nearest state university. Today, however, students often apply to ten or 15 colleges! At $25 for filing each application, that can be quite a hefty sum of money. (For students with very limited financial resources, this application fee will be waived.) College admissions people have no way of knowing which students are applying to a dozen or more colleges. In addition, applications are coming from students who, until recently, might not have considered a college education. And the "newcomers" are highly qualified because more and more people recognize that if they are going to be eligible for the higher paying jobs, they need that college diploma. Moreover, colleges and universities are actively recruiting minorities, students with disabilities, and foreign students. Bringing in bright, qualified students who once believed college was not within their reach is a very exciting prospect. It assures a greater diversity on college campuses and benefits everybody.

THE IMPORTANCE OF PLANNING

Many high school seniors are shocked to discover they have not been accepted into any college. Even students with terrific SATs and grades from excellent high schools can be left out in the cold, although by midsummer many of these students apply to a second round of colleges and find one to take them or decide to stop out for a year.

Once you have made the decision to go to college, you don't want to get caught in that bind. Here are some things you can do to get into the college you prefer:

1. Apply to your first-choice college well in advance of the deadline and ask for an early decision. This means that if you are accepted, you need look no further. You simply send in your nonreturnable deposit to hold your place. If you aren't accepted via early decision, you still have plenty of time to apply to other colleges.

2. Don't be afraid to choose a college that most of your friends have never heard of. If it meets your needs, then it is right for you.

3. Many colleges and universities actively seek students who are from a different population or part of the country than their average student. A qualified student from North Dakota, for example, who applies to an eastern university may be chosen over an equally qualified student from Scarsdale, New York. Don't be afraid to take chances.

4. Be sure to fill out each application carefully. Unless your handwriting is really excellent (or unless it is required that you handwrite your essay), use a computer or a typewriter with correction tape. Too much white-out makes you appear careless. Today, however, filing college applications has become much easier (and quicker) thanks to the Internet. Many, but not all, colleges accept a standard application form that can be found on the Internet. Do remember to be just as careful

using an electronic application form as you would with a handwritten or typed application. It is just as easy to make a mistake on an electronic form as it is with an application you hold in your hands.

Also, Apply Technology sponsors the Apply! (http://www.weapply.com) Web site where admissions applications from over 600 colleges and universities—from Alaska Pacific University to Michigan State to Yale University—are available as quickly as you can download and complete them. The best thing about Apply! is that it's free. And these aren't generic or Common applications but exact duplicates of each college's application form. In addition, Apply! offers direct links to the home pages of participating colleges, as well as general information—such as student demographics, tuition, and application deadlines—for hundreds of other colleges and universities.

Your personal essay may be the deciding factor in whether or not a college wants you. Admissions people carefully read every single essay. They are adept at figuring out if what you have written is truly yours. Write from the heart about something that matters to you. That can be more impressive than trying to sound falsely intellectual. It's fine to get advice on writing that essay, and by all means, have someone check your spelling. But be yourself. And if you are one of those rare people who can inject a little humor into your essay, it will help set you apart from other applicants.

5. Apply to as many colleges as you feel you need to, but be realistic in your expectations.

6. If you've been out of school for a couple of years, contact your high

> **"Your personal essay may be the deciding factor in whether or not a college wants you."**

school well in advance of the date your application is due. The guidance department is busy helping current students get ready for college. Getting your records out of the computer may not be top priority. Write or call your school to make sure your records are mailed out in time.

STRATEGY CAN BE IMPORTANT

Dan Wallner had determined that the only college he really wanted to attend was the University of California in Santa Cruz. It was the only one he applied to. As an out-of-state applicant, he didn't get in the first time, but he was determined to go there. So he plotted his strategy. First he moved to Santa Cruz and enrolled in their special summer program right after he graduated from high school. He threw himself into his course work and wrote an excellent final paper. His professor agreed to write a letter of recommendation when he reapplied. Next, he found an apartment, got a job, and established residency.

But Dan needed to know just why he'd been denied admission the first time, so he asked the admissions people what went wrong. He discovered his achievement test scores were 30 points below Santa Cruz's cut off. "I knew I'd blown off that test and had no doubt the second time around, I'd do much better," Dan says.

"I retook the ACT as soon as it was offered, scored 100 points higher than before, and submitted a new application, with a letter of reference from my summer school professor. I also enrolled in a couple of uni-

> "I knew I'd have to make myself known to the admissions people."

versity extension courses. But I was really worried. I started hearing that thousands of students were applying to Santa Cruz, and I thought, 'Oh, heck, I'm going to be just one of thousands.' I knew I'd have to make myself known to the admissions people."

Periodically, over the next months, Dan stopped in to speak to an admissions person. He checked with her to make sure all of his records and recommendations had arrived. He chatted about the courses he was taking in the Extension College and about how much it meant to him to study at this university. "I made it pretty clear that Santa Cruz was the only school for me. I guess it worked, because one day I got a phone call telling me 'unofficially' I was accepted, and I got the acceptance letter in the mail in a couple of days."

What to Do If You Don't Get into Your Favorite College

1. Write a polite letter to the admissions office asking for the specific reasons you were turned down.

2. Find out if it is possible to submit further information that might correct a wrong impression.

3. If there is a chance your application may be reconsidered, ask for an interview if you haven't already had one.

4. Find out if you can attend that college as a nonmatriculated student for a semester. If you can, work to get the best grades possible, then reapply.

5. If you find out you don't stand a chance to get in, then reassess your college choices, and apply to other colleges.

This was not an ordinary strategy, but it worked because Dan was very clear on what he wanted to do—and because he'd chosen a university that was realistically within his academic abilities.

So even if you blow your chances of getting into your first-choice college the first time around, if you are sure it's the right place for you, you can plan your life so that the next time you apply, you'll have a better chance to get in.

You Don't Have to Be On Campus to Get a College Degree

Today it is entirely possible to obtain a college degree without setting foot on a college campus. How? By signing up with a college or university that offers its courses via the Internet. Many fine universities have been offering courses on the Net for several years. Other colleges are just starting to go on line, and will offer some, but not all of their courses leading to a degree. And at some universities, professors put their lectures on the Net so that if a student has to miss a class, he or she can catch up. Or professors put specific questions on the Net and students can engage in discussions via "chat rooms"— or e-mail their professor with answers or with questions they may have about the assignment.

But why would you want to take an on line course rather than a course with a professor face-to-face in a real classroom with real students to interact with?

Perhaps you will be doing a semester or a year abroad and your favorite college professor is offering a course you especially want to take. You can take that course so long as you have a place to plug in your computer and access to the Web.

Or perhaps like Kristen Thomas, you cannot be on campus all the time. Taking courses on line while in another part of the country means you will be able to graduate in a reasonable amount of time without taking a leave of absence.

Shortly after Kristen graduated from high school, she married her high school sweetheart. Her husband joined the Marines, and Kristen followed him to Camp Lejune in North Carolina, where she became a full-time housewife and the mother of a son. The first time her husband was deployed overseas for six months, Kristen moved back with her son to Candor, New York, to stay with her mom, who offered to take care of her son. Kristen had decided it was time for her to think about a career in nursing for herself, but with a young child, this was going to be especially difficult when she rejoined her husband. "Then I heard about the Student Learning Network through Tompkins-Cortland Community College (TC-3)." Kristen discovered that she could take some of her courses at the community college during the months she was staying with her mother, and some of her courses on line when she was back in North Carolina—or wherever her husband was stationed.

"Sometimes you have computer problems, or the server is down or something like that."

"My nursing courses I will take face-to-face, but my SLN courses are basics. This is the first semester I'm doing the SLN courses, and," she notes, "it has had its ups and downs. It's good if the professor is very clear on what he or she wants. We've been having problems with one professor, though. This professor just tells you what to read and doesn't answer his e-mail, and also, he doesn't post discussion questions."

There can be other problems, too. "Sometimes you have computer problems, or the server is down or something like that. But, on balance, this is a great way for me to get my education. I'm always on the computer. I'm always checking my e-mail to see what my classmates have said in their discussions, and then I will reply to them." Kristen also likes the fact that while there are deadlines she has to meet, there is no set time for her to get on line.

"You know, when I was a student in high school, I goofed off a lot. But being away from home, with a son, I realized that I need my education, and it's hard to get this education and try to find good day care down here. The SLN courses are a godsend.

"It's just as if it were face-to-face. It's almost like chatting, only you can't see the person."

Kristen is one of many students getting part, if not all of her education on the Web. At New York University, for example, there are over 20,000 students enrolled in on line courses. According to Dr. Kathleen McKee, vice president of academic affairs at Neumann College, there still needs to be much research done on how well the Internet delivers education. "One thing we've already found out is that the success rate of people completing on line courses is 90 percent!"

NEW TECHNOLOGY REACHES INTO THE CLASSROOM

Distance learning doesn't only happen through the Internet. Some colleges, especially small colleges,

"One thing we've already found out is that the success rate of people completing online courses is 90 percent!"

have begun to offer classes to partner colleges through a process called Picture Tel. Dr. Rosalie Merenda, president of Neumann College in Pennsylvania, is very enthusiastic about using the new technology because it "is an opportunity to offer classes where there may not be enough students in one college. Technology offers a way to bring about diversity and quality. We need the technology as an option."

Neumann has entered into a partnership with Beaver College to offer certain elective courses via Picture Tel. Professor Bill Lynch is a professor of English at Neumann College. He teaches courses in English literature and film, and has been teaching for nearly 30 years. He loves the challenge of teaching using television. "It's rather like juggling with four or five different balls and trying to keep them up in the air. You have to deal with course content; you have to try to read the faces of the students in front of you, and get feedback from them as to what they understand, and you've got to do the same thing for the people on the other end. You've got students in two locations, and you function as a kind of director . . . as you handle the visuals in terms of pushing the right buttons to get the right camera."

Michael Criscuolo is majoring in English at Neumann College and takes the interactive TV course in theater with Dr. Lynch. "It's different and new, and very worthwhile," he says. "I especially like interacting with Joyce and John from Beaver College. They are older students—middle-aged folks—and it is nice to interact with them. Also we get to share our own experiences as we read the assignments. Older students have a different perspective from the younger students at Neumann. We're all around the same age—19 or 20. Joyce is also an English major, and she has read so much more than I have. I feel as if I'm working much harder in this class."

"It's different and new, and very worthwhile."

The downside to the interactive TV, however, is obvious to Michael. "During our break, the students who are in the same room with Professor Lynch can talk to him, but the students at Beaver College can't. And another problem is that when one of us presents an oral report, there is an echo on our end, and that's disconcerting. Finally, those at Beaver have only one monitor. We have two. So if the professor is using the overhead, they can only see what's on that screen. They can hear, but they can't see anything else."

Dr. Merenda recognizes that interactive TV and on line courses offer many challenges. "Not all of the paradigms will work. Technology offers wonderful options, and we are taking baby steps here. There is a lot to learn."

The exciting thing for you as a college student in the 21st century is that you have options that no other generation of young people have had in the way you can pursue your own education. The most important thing you can do for yourself is to be aware of your strengths and weaknesses—and be honest about them. Don't put yourself down. But don't puff yourself up. College can be a grand adventure. Not only will you meet wonderful people, encounter ideas and subjects that you never dreamed about, and learn how to think and reason, but you will also be giving yourself a gift that is yours forever. No one can ever take away your education. It is the single experience that pays dividends over your entire lifetime and can provide you with untold years of pleasure.

LOOKING THROUGH LISTS AND LISTS OF COLLEGES CAN BE A DAUNTING UNDER-TAKING. With so many choices, it's not surprising that many people get frustrated and confused. The 1999 *Peterson's Guide to Four-Year Colleges,* for example, lists over 2,500 colleges. Barron's lists over 1,500. I hope some of the colleges mentioned throughout this book will be worth exploring. The addresses for some of the early admission colleges—PEG at Mary Baldwin, Simon's Rock College of Bard, The Clarkson School at Clarkson University, the TAMS at the University of North Texas, TALH at Lamar University, and the Advanced Academy of Georgia—are listed in Chapter VIII. Several people I interviewed mentioned some unusual colleges, as well. I'm including a highly selective and personal list of colleges for you to think about. Some I chose because they demand something very specific from students. I looked for colleges that address specific minority concerns—schools that are totally handicapped accessible, schools that have strong programs in African American Studies or Latin American Affairs, or schools with specific programs for students with learning disabilities. I hope I've chosen some overlooked treasures in our vast system of higher education. Perhaps one of these will be right for you.

1. Appalachian State University, Boone, North Carolina 28608, Phone: 828/262-2000, Web site: http://www.appstate.edu/. A small liberal arts college that is part of the state university system. Within the university is Watauga College which attracts about 100 students who live and study apart from the rest of the university. Those enrolled at Watauga design their own major fields of study.

2. Colorado College, Colorado Springs, Colorado 80903, E-mail: admissions@ColoradoCollege.edu, Web site: http://www.coloradocollege.edu/. The academic year is divided into eight blocks of time, each lasting three and a half weeks. During each block of time students concentrate on a single course. Students may design their own majors, and there are concentrations in such areas as African American, Asian, Latin American and Urban Studies.

3. Embry-Riddle Aeronautical University, Daytona Beach, Florida 32114-3900, E-mail (admissions): admit@db.erau.edu, Web site: http://www.embryriddle.edu/. A unique university that is located at Daytona Beach Regional Airport. There is a second campus in Prescott, Arizona. Undergraduate degree programs are in aviation education, including pilot training.

4. New College of the University of South Florida, 5700 North Tamiami Trail, Sarasota, Florida 34243, Phone: 941/359-4200, E-mail (admissions): ncadmissions@virtu.sar.usf.edu, Web site: http://www.newcollege.usf.edu/. The campus, which overlooks Sarasota Bay, is situated on the grounds of the former Ringling Brothers estate. The college has strong programs in the liberal arts, including environmental studies, English, fine and performing arts, philosophy, math, and sciences. Students receive written evaluations instead of grades. They are encouraged to design their own majors. All students are required to do independent studies.

5. College of the Atlantic, Bar Harbor, Maine 04609, Web site: http://www.coa.edu/. It's devoted to the study of ecology. Situated on a grand old estate on scenic Frenchman's Bay, it is within walking distance of the Atlantic Ocean and Acadia National Park. Students design their own programs within the areas of environmental design, environmental sciences, human studies, and public policy.

6. Cornish College of the Arts, 710 East Roy Street, Seattle, Washington 98102, Phone: 206/323-1400. Located in the heart of Seattle, Cornish Institute focuses on the arts—ceramics, sculpture, design, and dance. Students have to find their own housing, since the college isn't a residential one. Special attention is paid to students who are differently-abled, especially those in wheelchairs: lowered telephones, specially equipped restrooms.

7. World College West, 101 South San Antonio Road, Petaluma, California 94952. The average age of the students at World College West is 20 years. All first-year courses are team taught and interdisciplinary. Second-year students may study and work in either Nepal or Mexico. Third-year students may study in China. This experimental college places emphasis on academic study and cooperative governance. Study abroad—though optional—is encouraged. The academic year is divided into four 12-week quarters. Students study full time for two quarters and work in paying jobs for two.

8. Earlham College, Richmond, Indiana 47374-4095, Phone: 800/327-5426, Web site: http://www.earlham.edu/. This college was established by the Society of Friends, but is nonsectarian. Students are encouraged to design their own programs and take part in any one of the 27 programs offered in foreign countries. Virtually the entire campus is handicapped-accessible.

9. Goshen College, 1700 South Main Street, Goshen, Indiana 46526, Phone: 219/535-7000, E-mail: info@goshen.edu, Web site: http://www.goshen.edu/. Founded by the Mennonite Church, this college offers a study-service trimester abroad, 14 weeks of work and study. Requires international studies for graduation. Campus is equipped with wheelchair ramps and elevators, and can provide sign language courses and interpreters for the hearing impaired.

10. Palm Beach Atlantic College, PO Box 24708, West Palm Beach, Florida 33416-4708, Phone: 888/GO-TO-PBA, Web site: http://www.pbac.edu/. The centerpiece of this college is its educational philosophy called "Workship." Workship requires each full-time student to donate at least 200 hours of his or her time to community service over a four-year period. The college is affiliated with the Southern Baptist Convention, and most students are Baptists.

11. Shimer College, PO Box A500, Waukegan, Illinois 60079, Phone: 847/623-8400, E-mail: shimeradmin@shimer.edu, Web site: http://www.shimer.edu/. This college offers early admission to qualified students who have not completed high school. Core curriculum centers around the Great Books of the Western World, but students may create their own majors.

12. Howard University, 2400 Sixth Street, NW, Washington, DC 20059, Phone: 202/806-6100, E-mail: admission@howard.edu, Web site: http://www.howard.edu/. This college's special mission is to make higher education available to African American students. Virtually the entire campus is handicapped accessible for wheelchair-bound students. Counselors are available to help students with other handicapping conditions.

13. Gallaudet University, 800 Florida Avenue, NE, Washington, DC 20002-3695, Web site: http://www.gallaudet.edu/. This is the only private liberal arts college for the deaf. Offers an intensive one-year pre-college remedial program for students with academic deficiencies.

14. Alverno College, 3401 South 39th Street, PO Box 343922, Milwaukee, Wisconsin 53234-3922, Phone: 800/933-3401, Web site: http://www.alverno.edu/. This is a small Roman Catholic women's college that prides itself on its pioneering attitude in how students are assessed. Students must demonstrate competence in eight 'abilities,'—communication, analysis, problem solving, valuing, social interaction, global perspectives, effective citizenship, and aesthetic response. Courses are pass/fail, with oral and written feedback from faculty.

15. Texas A&M University at Galveston, PO Box 1675, Galveston, Texas 77553, Phone: 800/850-6376, E-mail: bellr@tamug.tamu.edu, Web site: http://www.tamug.tamu.edu/. This small liberal arts and science college boasts that "the ocean is our classroom." Situated on beautiful Galveston Island, it overlooks the *Elissa*, a restored 1877 tall ship. TAMUG offers degrees in marine biology, marine fisheries, oceanography, maritime administration, and many other majors having to do with the sea. In addition, students can elect to sit for a Merchant Marine exam upon graduation, and earn either a Third Mate's deck license or a Third Assistant Engineer's license. Or they may train for the U.S. Coast Guard Reserve or U.S. Naval Reserve. Part of their training is done on the *Texas Clipper II,* a former U.S. Navy vessel. Entering college freshmen can take their first college credits at sea.

Sometimes a two-year or community college will be just what you are looking for, especially for students who have stopped out for a while or those who need to upgrade their academic skills. Your own local community college may offer the opportunity to get back into the swing of academic life. Some offer intensive English as a Second Language courses, others unique programs leading to an associate of arts or science degree that can't be obtained anywhere else. Three which I found particularly intriguing are:

1. **Bel Rea Institute of Animal Technology,** 1681 South Dayton, Denver, Colorado 80231, Phone: 800/950-8001, E-mail: admissions@bel-rea.com, Web site: http://www.bel-rea.com/. The Institute offers an associate's degree in animal technology. Courses run for six consecutive quarters, including summers for 18 months. Students attend classes for five quarters and take part in a paid internship program during the sixth quarter. The degree prepares them for para-professional work in veterinary medicine.

2. **Culinary Institute of America,** 433 Albany Post Road, Hyde Park, New York 12538, Phone: 914/452-9600, Web site: http://www.ciachef.edu/. CIA awards an associate degree in culinary arts and baking and pastry arts, and bachelor degree programs in culinary arts management and baking and pastry arts management. The

program operates through the year with new classes starting every three weeks—16 times a year. Students get hands-on experience in cooking and baking as well as theoretical knowledge that underlies competence in both fields. Students also work at paid internships.

3. Navajo Community College, Tsaile, Arizona 86556, and PO Box 580, Shiprock, New Mexico 876420, E-mail (admissions): louise@crystal.ncc.cc.nm.us, Web site: http://crystal.ncc.cc.nm.us/. This is the first Indian-owned and operated college in the United States. Begun in both Arizona and New Mexico in 1968, Navajo Community College offers numerous associate of arts degrees including one in Navajo bilingual education.

AMONG THE MOST USED BOOKS IN ANY LIBRARY ARE THOSE WHICH DESCRIBE COL-LEGES AND UNIVERSITIES. You can always spot them because the covers quickly get battered through constant usage. Here are some that you may want to browse through. Most of these are revised frequently.

American Universities and Colleges, Washington: American Council on Education. Describes approximately 2,200 accredited institutions.

Barron's Guide to the Most Prestigious Colleges. Westbury, NY: Barron's Educational Services. Profiles several hundred colleges and universities with the highest entrance standards.

Chronicle Four-Year College Data Book. Moravia, NY. Chronicle Guidance Publications. Summarizes information on approximately 2,000 four-year colleges.

College Blue Book. New York. Macmillan Publishing Company. A five-volume set which includes descriptions of colleges and universities and financial aid offerings.

The College Handbook. New York. The College Board. Summarizes information on 3,000 two- and four-year colleges.

The College Money Handbook. Princeton. Peterson's Guides. Cites costs at four-year colleges and provides background information on the financial aid process.

Community Junior and Technical College Directory. Washington. American Association of Community and Junior Colleges. Describes accredited two-year colleges.

Comparative Guide to American Colleges. New York. Harper & Row. Describes and briefly evaluates accredited institutions.

Global Guide to International Education. New York. Facts on File Publications. Cites opportunities for overseas study in 150 countries.

Index of Majors. New York. The College Board. Lists approximately 400 majors and tells which colleges offer them.

The Insider's Guide to Colleges. New York. St. Martin's Press. Developed by the *Yale Daily News.* Presents the students' view of various colleges and universities.

National College Databank. Princeton. Peterson's Guides. Groups colleges to help students pinpoint institutions of particular interest.

Peterson's Competitive Colleges. Princeton. Peterson's Guides. Describes approximately 300 colleges with high admissions standards.

Peterson's Guide to Colleges with Programs for Learning Disabled Students. Princeton. Peterson's Guides. Describes colleges for special needs students.

Peterson's Guide to Four-Year Colleges. Princeton. Peterson's Guides. Describes accredited colleges and universities.

Peterson's Guide to Two-Year Colleges. Princeton. Peterson's Guides. Profiles approximately 1,400 two-year colleges.

For Parents, Only

THIS IS THE ONLY SECTION IN THE BOOK NOT DIRECTED TO STUDENTS. Instead, it is an open letter to your parents.

Dear Mom and Dad,

Being a conscientious parent of teenage kids today is probably almost as difficult as being a teenager. Our kids live in a world not of their making. More dangerous stuff is readily available to young people today than there ever was when we were their age. They are constantly faced with difficult choices we never had to consider: drugs, alcohol, lethal weapons, an increasingly polluted environment, a rapidly changing economy, and technology that is changing the way we study and work almost daily. Our concept of family life is also undergoing vast changes. Both we and our children often have to deal with painful situations that were completely unknown to older generations.

In addition to trying to cope with all the forces outside of themselves, today's youth are grappling with the same big questions we and our parents and grandparents dealt with: Who am I? What do I really believe in? Do I look all right? Am I attractive (or handsome) enough to attract that guy or gal sitting next to me? Do my parents love me? Am I in control of my life? Am I making the right choice? What's the purpose of my life? Will I be able to get a job when I'm through with school?

What may be the biggest surprise is that despite all of the stresses and the unknowns, our children have an incredible spirit of adventure.

They are ready and willing to take some risks early in their lives because they sense that when they are older, those opportunities might not be available to them.

Perhaps the most difficult thing parents of teenagers have to cope with is their children's passion. Most 16- and 17-year-olds aren't often very adept at presenting a cogent and well-thought-out argument, especially to the people who mean the most—Mom and Dad. When kids discuss their plans with their friends, it all seems to make good sense. When the same kid tries to explain to a parent why he or she wants to work for a year or two, or study abroad, the words tend to tumble out in unintended abruptness. What begins as a discussion can quickly turn to anger, and can end in a failure of understanding on both sides.

I guess we all have some sort of notion of what we'd like our children to do and be. We want them to move ahead with a good education, a secure future, and a lot of joy and happiness. There probably isn't a parent alive who doesn't want his or her child to avoid youthful mistakes. Yet we all know that no child grows up without making decisions that have turned out to be wrong, without arguing with parents, without striking out on his or her own. My writing teacher used to remind her class that without conflict, there is no story. And in real life, without conflict, a person doesn't change and grow.

Several parents whose children were interviewed for this book were kind enough to share their feelings about the paths their offspring had taken.

Robert Sigmon's daughter, Kiran, took time out between high school and college to join other young people on special projects in New Zealand and China. Kiran earned all of her travel money on her own. Mr. Sigmon, who is the associate director of an outreach education program at Wake Medical Center in Raleigh, North Carolina, is delighted with the challenges Kiran sought out. "Although it is partly genetic," he says, not all together jokingly. "Her mother, whose parents were missionaries in China, and I actually met in Pakistan. What is especially gratifying is that Kiran accepted the responsibility for what she's doing. I think she'll land on her feet . . . A lot of parents asked me how I could have let her go off like that—and my answer is I didn't let her go. She just went. All kids should have their own odyssey between the ages of 16 and 20."

"Sure, I had secret fears, which I didn't announce in public," says Rebecca Godin, whose son, Sam, left college to join a band. "But I supported Sam's decision because the kids in the band needed to strike while the iron was hot. They had just won this fabulous trip to Japan. They really had to take that chance. You know, I don't believe that college has to be a four-year lock-step. Life isn't like that. Just because a person is in college, he or she shouldn't feel they can't take hold of an unusual opportunity when it comes along." Despite Rebecca's concern that Sam might decide on the very unpredictable life of a traveling musician, she also had enough faith in his desire to complete his education. She wasn't wrong. "Parents have to be willing to trust that they've imparted values that are important to them," she says. "And education has always been important in our family."

My plea to parents is to set aside your notions of what you want for your kids, and really listen to what they are saying. Some of their ideas and goals may sound totally naive, even crazy. And you may be tempted to tell them so. Don't. Let them talk. Some of their hopes and dreams may break your heart in their simple yearning. Some of those desires may touch your own hidden dreams, and you may be astounded to find how much like you your children really are—or how much like a half-forgotten member of your family.

I interviewed literally dozens of young people for this book. Each was simply wonderful to talk with. They were full of plans and full of life. They were thrilled that I wanted to know what they'd done.

They were honored that I wanted to know how they figured things out. Some of them confess that after talking to me, they'd decided to make some changes in their plans. Those young people who had stopped out for a year or two before going on to college had such a marvelous sense of purpose. One of my respondents had stayed out of school for four years—and I know that his parents were fearful that he'd never go to college. Yet, once he made up his mind, he went through a five-year undergraduate and MBA program in three years. Today he is an accountant, married, and lives in Philadelphia.

All kids are not alike. They learn in different ways and at different rates. We all recognize this in little children—why should we expect our teens to be any different?

If your children complain about not learning anything in high school—listen to what they are saying. Maybe they've gotten all they can out of the place. They, better than anyone else, know what they are capable of. Give them a chance. If going to college early is what they really want to do, encourage them. Explore the options. Don't let young minds wither in an uninteresting and mind-deadening high school setting. On the other hand, take care not to push them into early college. And, let your child know that if it doesn't work out, that's OK, too. There really are lots of options out there, and lots of things to try.

And what if your son or daughter has been a mediocre student, or has been labeled "learning disabled"? Or has other disabilities? That child who has not been successful in a traditional school for whatever reasons, has innate gifts and abilities that need to be uncovered. What you can do as a parent is to show that you have enough faith in your kid to seek out a school that will help him or her reach that potential that is there. Don't give up on your child.

I believe the more you treat teenagers with trust and respect, the more they will take up the challenge to act in responsible ways. You may say, "Yeah, sure. But you don't know my kid." And that is perfectly true. But as a person who has spent a major part of her adult life teaching and writing about kids and education (and whose own three kids provided moments of high and low drama), I do know that the more you try to push certain kinds of young people into a mold, the more they will rebel. The sooner teenagers have the opportunity to make decisions for themselves, the sooner they will be in control of their own lives—and take responsibility for their successes and their failures.

The reward for encouraging your children to make their own choices, and giving them enough help to allow them to be successful, is that the trust and respect you offer gets returned—albeit later. Sometimes much later. Hang in there. It is worth it.

I hope this modest book will help your son or daughter make some important decisions about their future—and that you will find it within yourselves to support their choices.

Sincerely,

Bryna J. Fireside

INDEX